EDUCATION FOR CHANGE

EDUCATION
for CHANGE

Joseph D. Ban

THE JUDSON PRESS
Valley Forge

EDUCATION FOR CHANGE

CONTENTS

INTRODUCTION

HOW MAY WE EDUCATE PERSONS to live and minister in times of tremendous change? This timely question is the concern of this book. We are not concerned with change for its own sake but with change that builds—with change as it relates to learning, and with learning as it relates to change.

There are many books about the tremendous changes of our decade, but this one has a special reason for being. It is written from the vantage point that God has made known his purpose in Jesus Christ. It assumes that God intends Christ's followers to fulfill the divine purpose through effective ministry suited to each period of the world's history. It is concerned with this ministry in whatever forms the changing conditions of our day may require.

Education for such ministry begins with Christ's commission. As the church in obedience to him carries out its mission in the world, it establishes the context for its educational ministry. In this world of rapid change God is at work, and here the church must be.

This book interprets an entirely new approach to curriculum planning, which is discussed in the later chapters. In the earlier chapters, however, the big picture of a world in change is painted in swift strokes, and we are introduced to the idea that God's hand moves in change. Both in the Bible and in current experience we see evidence of God at work bringing about change and creating meaningful order within change.

Logically, then, we must ask searching questions about man's part in all of these changes. Is man just a puppet, or does he have a responsible part in fashioning change? The chapters entitled "Mission Amidst Revolution" and "Shapers of Change" are both addressed to this vital issue.

In Chapter 5 we are introduced to a teaching-learning concept keyed to this world of change. It represents the most significant development to emerge in present-day curriculum planning. In the past, curriculum planners and writers have tended to emphasize either the *tradition* (as in Bible-centered materials) or the *learner* (as in child-centered approaches). Neither of these emphases, however, is adequate in itself for our day. The new curriculum plan is new precisely because it provides for teaching-learning experiences related to both emphases. These are made possible through the concept of the *crossing point,* which takes into account the content of the Christian faith as well as the context of the learner at his own particular point of development as a person. The crossing point thus represents the intersection of the learner's persisting life concerns with the dynamic of the gospel.

If it is true that today's world is experiencing changes vastly greater than those encountered by earlier generations, then the church confronts a great new challenge as it identifies specific crossing points in the lives of its people. How to respond to that challenge, therefore, is examined in Chapters 6 and 7, "Love in Learning" and "Christian Education as Experience." Here the case for love in relation to the learning tasks is carefully presented.

Chapter 8, "Rendezvous for Mission," opens for our consideration some of the ways in which the congregation educates for mission. For example, a study of worship in the educational life of the Christian fellowship leads directly to a recognition of some crossing points at various stages in the life span. We see also the pastor's important role as teacher of teachers, and we consider the meaning of the teaching-learning group.

The next chapter, "Education for Living," is concerned with the main features of a specific curriculum plan, based on the Cooperative Curriculum Project. Recognizing the necessity of preparing Christians for decisive living in the midst of change, curriculum planners have offered specific curriculum resources to help carry out this essential task of Christian education.

The concluding chapter is more personal. What kind of person is the hoped-for product of any curriculum for Christian nurture? In the entirely new context for the presentation of the gospel which modern change has created, the Christian is called to develop a new style of life. He who dares to live responsibly in the midst of revolution will need to pioneer in a new way of being. In a sense, this chapter is a challenge to a new piety.

Education for Change does not pretend to be the final and authoritative word on curriculum planning. It has been written, however, because the author firmly believes that modern man stands in great need of the joyous news that liberty—true liberty—is made possible through the love of Christ. New ways of sharing this truth can help many more persons enter into a teaching and learning experience where the gospel breaks through into their own personal situations. Christian education can prepare men and women for decisive living in times of change.

The author writes out of his experience with the Cooperative Curriculum Project and the American Baptist—Disciples of Christ "cluster" for curriculum development. The American Baptists refer to their curriculum design and resources as the Christian Faith and Work Plan while the Disciples of Christ call theirs the Christian Life Curriculum. The discussion in these pages of curriculum planning is related to both of these, and applies in general to all denominational developments which have grown out of the Cooperative Curriculum Project. These include: Church of the Brethren, Encounter Series; Church of God, Ventures in Christian Living; and the Canadian Baptists, All-Canada Baptist Publications.

1 *LIFE IS CHANGE*

OTHER THAN CHRISTMAS, perhaps there is no more exciting time around the house than the week before school opens. The children have notebooks to buy and pencil boxes to fill while Mother checks on the lunch boxes and the rain gear. The most exciting part is trying on the clothes that fitted so nicely last fall. Now, a year later, the sleeves are too skimpy and the length is too short, not to mention other parts that are filled out. The check-writing part of Daddy shudders, but the rest of him rejoices at the look on his child's face: "Look, Daddy, how I have grown!" We have only to watch a child grow in wisdom and stature to appreciate the importance of change.

To live means to change. Everybody experiences minor changes continually, and each day holds the possibility of radical change. Change marks the times we remember best—whether the happy moment when we met the person with whom we were to share life most intimately, or the tragic hour when we lost a loved one. Change is the new taking the place of the old. Change involves variety: new and different conditions altering and substituting for what formerly prevailed. Change is the essence of life.

Change does not always come smoothly or easily. A Christian leader recalls the beauty of those rare days in his youth when the great Ohio River was frozen over. Snow covered the land and the ice-locked river. There was a peaceful quietness over the earth. Then came the day of the spring thaw. Loud explosions rocked the calm as the crystalline white beauty was replaced by dull grays and muddy browns. But the people of the valley did not resent the passing of the old with its beauty and its peace, for they knew that after the thaw would come the green growth of spring.[1]

The experience of change is often like that. A world of beauty laid out in order and majesty (or so it seems) suddenly begins to break up. We sense that a better time may be ahead, but for now at least, all is in noisy confusion. Many of us, however, do not readily accept change. Rather, we may resist it, preferring the known to the unknown. Though what we have may not be too satisfactory, at least we know what it is and we have learned to live with it. Eric Hoffer recalls his experience as a migrant worker moving from the task of picking peas, as the season changed, to picking string beans. "Even the change from peas to string beans had in it elements of fear," he comments.[2]

Even so, however, change is inescapable in present-day living. Today, for instance, even a family that resides in a stable community must face the fact that the sons and daughters are likely to move away. They may spend their maturing years at a distant college or with the armed forces on a faraway military base. They may become employed by a corporation that transfers its personnel frequently from place to place. Or they may just move frequently from town to town looking for a better job. As the years go by, it becomes less and less likely that our children will "stay put" in the place of their birth.

If change is so important, why do we find it uncomfortable? In part, because fixed patterns are as necessary for living as are the dynamics of change. In order not to go through the same procedures of decision-making every day, we must organize our lives. To avoid repetitious decisions, we develop routines for handling daily needs. These are called habits. The housewife relies on the tried-and-true recipe. The businessman leans heavily on the "usual way" to do business. Society as a whole develops informal practices called customs and often codifies these into regulations and laws. Thus we develop comfortable patterns which spare us the need for repeated decision.

It is important to recognize that this process of organizing life is as essential as the constant need for change. We need both form and vitality. Organization seeks to provide one essential, and change yields the other. This is not to suggest that all organization is static and all change is creative. Indeed, history provides clear evidence that institutions can organize for change and that revolutions (radical efforts at change) can set progress back.[2]

CHANGE HAS ACCELERATED

We sometimes assume that our generation is the first to confront change. But think back upon your own grandparents and their predecessors. If they were farmers, think of the changeable factors in their ordinary day. The weather was always unpredictable. When to cut, dry, and store hay varied from one year to the next. The market for their foodstuffs changed constantly. The model T, new tar roads, and rural electricity revolutionized their way of life, bringing new opportunities and introducing new problems. Thus what on the surface appears as a tranquil pastoral scene reveals on closer examination a continuous atmosphere of change. Obviously, change is not new.

What is new for our generation is the acceleration of change. People of previous generations often had a lifetime to adjust to a major change. When plenty of time was available, even vast changes like the dissolution of the Roman Empire, the growth of towns and cities, the decline of feudalism, the development of gunpowder, and the invention of the printing press could be taken in stride. To be sure, each of these changes shocked the standing system, but the people had many years to live with the new situation before another change came along. It has been said that whereas once it took several generations to encompass one social or cultural change, now it takes several cultural or social changes to make up one generation.

In order to understand the acceleration of change in our own times, let us examine as an example the change in the communication field. From the time of Abraham to the invention of the printing press, man was essentially dependent on the *oral* process of communication. Practically everything was passed on from person to person and from generation to generation by words spoken, heard, and memorized. Later there was writing, first on stones, then on reed-paper (papyrus), and then on parchment. There were also some libraries, but for the most part books (scrolls) were ornaments enjoyed by the wealthy nobles or endowed monasteries. Bibles were chained to the pulpits in the Middle Ages for the same reason today's motel owners bolt color TV sets to the wall: These items represent valuable property easily sold on the illicit market.

The invention of movable type made *literary* man possible. Man began to use the written word as his primary method of communication. The printing press made a great treasury of written works available to the average man. It made possible the widespread interest in reading which popularized the works of Shakespeare, the King James Bible, and Samuel Johnson's dictionary, and continues in our own day.

Today we confront a new revolution: mass *visual* media, chiefly evident in the form of motion pictures and television. As once man moved across the threshold from the *spoken* word to the *written* word, so now we cross to *seeing* the event. The television screen is dramatic proof of the emergence of a new period in the history of communications. Its impact became especially evident in the course of the Vietnam war. In all previous wars the average citizen had depended on rumors (word of mouth), or newspaper stories (written words), or pictures (Matthew Brady's Civil War photographs), or motion pictures of the battle action. With the outbreak of war in Vietnam, however, such scenes as napalm bombing, maimed children, and Viet Cong atrocities began to appear on the TV screen. Whether this development leads to a more sensitive involvement of the people or to a numbing of their senses is a question still to be answered. Some observers think it may be used as a form of thought control. George Orwell's novel *Nineteen Eighty-Four* provides a pessimistic prediction of technology undermined by political tyranny.

Notice how rapidly change has accelerated in the field of communication. Many thousands of years elapsed between Abraham and Gutenberg. But it was only a few hundred years from the printing press to the radio, and only a quarter-century from that stage to television. And along with the electronics revolution has come a breathtaking series of other changes in such fields as air travel, nuclear power, computers, modern medicine, and political development (emergence of new nations).

British economist Barbara Ward, summarizing ten or twenty revolutions of catastrophic proportions, has isolated four as most significant in our fast-changing times. These are (1) the revolution of equality, (2) the revolution of this-worldliness (the idea of progress by material change to a better world here and now, rather than hereafter), (3) a biological revolution (the sudden vast increase in the rate at which the human race is multiplying), and (4) the application of science to nearly all aspects of living.[4]

Technological revolution has brought about extraordinary changes in every modern nation, especially in the emerging nations. The violent political revolutions in Russia and China have produced extensive changes in the structure of society, but no more so than the gradual revolution of technology in England, the Scandinavian countries, and North America, where governments and people were more flexible in their adjustment to change, and the social class structure was more open to upward societal movements of workers. In the United States an economy has developed which allows both management and labor to share in the benefits of technological production.

The American economy in recent generations has seen a move from the mechanized assembly line to an even more efficient form of manufacturing in which electronic circuits control production. There is no longer any problem of producing enough goods to meet the people's needs. Instead, we are seeing a growing emphasis on consumption of goods as contrasted with production. More leisure is available to the worker under various plans such as sabbaticals for steelworkers, four-day work weeks, etc. And still the revolution continues. Now the automated assembly line is being tied together with the computer's vast storage of data, making possible an automatic processing from the raw goods of the farmer's fields to the housewife's shopping basket in the supermarket. We are just beginning to recognize the vast impact upon our way of life as automation is linked to the computer. This new development is called by the term *cybernation,* a big word in the future of us all.[5]

Such technological advances may be either a blessing or a curse, depending on how we use them. A Christian ecumenical study conference saw in technology the possibilities of conquering mankind's enemies of poverty, hunger, and disease. "Technology provides the fundamental hope for the liberation of mankind from poverty and disease," the report stated. "Economic and political organization play an important part in the eradication of poverty, but the tools they use involve the powers of technology."[6]

Where technology helps to wipe out poverty and provide social mobility, it gives man dignity, freedom, and health. The Christian welcomes such advances as these. In other situations, however, the values of change are less certain. Radical changes in family values or in community and social structures can be traced to the impact of technology. Sometimes these lead to a better world, sometimes not. In such situations Christians have a responsibility to interpret the gospel in such a way as to assist their fellowmen in finding wholesome ways of living.

The need to provide consumers for the products of automation has led to some unfortunate personality-debasing practices in much of contemporary advertising. Man is represented to the average television viewer as a patched-together collection of sniffles, heartburn, throbbing headaches, and intestinal disorders—no part of his life is intimate enough to escape the huckster who now uses motivation research to land him as a customer. Our economy is tampering with human personality. No emotion is too delicate, no personal problem too serious to be exploited by some stranger in pursuit of a profit. As a "salesman of the year" told a realtors' association, "If you go out and make people dissatisfied with [the home] they have, you're going to have more sales and you're going to make people happy." [7]

CHANGE AFFECTS OUR WAY OF LIVING

Now let us look at the process of change from a different perspective. The history of the past one hundred years in the United States illustrates change as it has influenced community and personal life patterns.

In colonial days American life was based upon an agricultural economy typified by the small New England town, with sheep grazing on a village green surrounded by homes, and with the villagers' farms in the outlying area. The Revolutionary War ushered in the first major change, development of commerce and industry, and the Civil War created the image of life in a small town that we still like to recall. In this picture we see the village square with its monument to a soldier or a volunteer fireman. Around the square are the churches, a few stores, and perhaps a public building. On the edge of the town stands a mill, and beyond it lie the farmers' fields. In such a small town most of "the folks" know each other by name. A man is identified by his trade or his skill as a farmer, and family ties are strong. "That's Tom Edwards' oldest boy. His dad has that fine herd of dairy cows." The townspeople watch the children grow up, marry, and establish their own homes in the same community.

There were good things about life in that nineteenth-century small town. The man at the furniture store would never sell you more furniture than you needed, because he more than likely knew just how much you could afford. Besides, it was unlikely that any self-respecting citizen would go to him without having enough cash on hand to pay for his purchase. Personal relationships were developed over many years and tended to have depth. In Small Town, U.S.A., everyone had a place. Identity was tied in with his job, and the locales of his work, his residence, and his leisure were largely identical.[*]

Along with these good qualities the small town also had some drawbacks. Class lines were easily drawn. The man who worked at the factory, for example, carried his lunch pail and did not see his family at all during the day. In contrast, the business or professional man would draw the shade down over the office door and walk home at noon to enjoy his luncheon with his family and possibly take a short nap before he returned to his work.

A hundred years later, in the latter part of the twentieth century, only a small percentage of Americans now expect to spend their entire lifetimes in small towns. Except for these few, the intimate neighbor-to-neighbor relationships accumulated through generations of living in the same community are gone. In much of modern America the tradesman or serviceman is a stranger to you, and you naturally develop suspicions regarding the quality of his goods and services and the honesty of his bill. Your neighbor may not even know where you work or what you do. In fact, even your own family may not have a clear picture of your job. A cartoon showed two little boys talking. Said one lad, "I don't know where my daddy works. All I know is that he said it makes him sick to his stomach."

Living under such conditions, we have ever so many acquaintances but altogether too few friends. We live in one place, work in another, worship at yet another, and relax somewhere else. Each of these locations offers a different, but incomplete, set of interpersonal relationships. Each group of persons becomes acquainted with only a part of us.[*]

Sensitive parents are concerned about how best to prepare their children to live in times of change, and the church school shares this concern. The function of the church's educational ministry at all times is to help in the process of allowing personalities to grow. Today in particular, this growth needs to be in the direction of the strength-stability and alert flexibility which a rapidly changing society requires. The teaching ministry of the church can help to meet this need.

A PARALLEL FROM BIBLE TRADITIONS

Fortunately the church can draw effectively upon the Bible for light upon our own experiences with radical change. The Old Testament, for instance, with its history of the people of ancient Israel, can illuminate some aspects of modern living. From the days of Abraham to those of King Saul we see almost a thousand years of nomadic or seminomadic existence in which the families depend upon grazing animals for a living. Examples of this may be seen in the stories of Abraham and Lot (Genesis 11—25) and Joseph and his brothers (Genesis 30—50).

The change from a grasslands nomadic economy to a settled agricultural economy began to develop as the Jewish migrants under Joshua settled in Canaan. It continued over many years, roughly covering the period of the champions (judges) of Israel (Judges 2:16). The transition from nomadic grazing to settled farming is reflected in the story of Samuel's anointing of Saul as the future king, because the herd of asses which Saul had set out to fetch were obviously domesticated animals. Furthermore, Saul's father, Kish, is portrayed as a well-to-do farmer with good landholdings (1 Samuel 9, 10).

The change to the next stage beyond farming is seen in the story of David, the great king whose reign represents the high-water mark of Israel. David's personal history begins with his experiences as a shepherd boy (1 Samuel 16:11), and we see him rise from rural herding to urban life in a city which he has captured and made into the national center of Israel's cultural, political, and religious life. In contrast to this is the life story of his son Solomon, born and reared in all the opulence of an oriental potentate's court. Consider the vast difference in the early lives of these two kings!

ABRAHAM	MOSES Exodus	SAUL	DAVID	SOLOMON
c. 2000 B.C.	c. 1300 B.C	c. 1030 B.C.	c. 1000 B.C.	c. 960 B.C.

ECONOMY:
grazing ⟶ farming ⟶ city (commerce)

CULTURE:
simple life ⟶ courtly life
folk stories ⟶ psalms

SIMPLICITY ⟶ COMPLEXITY

The simple chart illustrates some factors of change.[10] Note the increasing complexity as change occurs. In the nomadic way of life a man could start his own business with a tent and a few sheep. In fact, Abraham and Lot did just that (Genesis 13:1-12), settling their differences easily as one simply allowed the other to choose where his herds would pasture. Contrast the simple economics of these nomadic chieftains with the more complex financial arrangements required a few hundred years later for the simplest of farms. Even in those early times, a farmer needed a large capital investment in land, seed, tools, grain sacks, draft animals, and buildings.

Why the movement from the free and open life of the nomad to the more complex, more difficult, and more restrictive life of the farm village? In practical terms, the nomad gave up his mobility because the farmer was more certain to eat regularly. For the wandering shepherd it was feast or famine, depending on the availability and condition of the water holes and on the number of tribes competing for the same grasslands. For the farmer, regular harvests replaced these uncertainties. Now he could store his food for year-round use, build a house, and join in the life of a community.[11]

The thousand years from Abraham to Solomon brought vast socioeconomic change. Solomon, who is as notable for his extravagant taste as he is for wisdom, depleted the resources of the nation by excessive expenditures and set the stage for the north-south split of the kingdom and the gradual eclipse of the once-powerful state. Yet at the same time his cosmopolitan reign allowed the development of a new and fairly sophisticated culture.

Thus Old Testament history demonstrates that the Bible itself records a process of change similar to that which characterizes the modern situation. But this is not all. The New Testament also is a story of change. In fact, one of the Christmas narratives tells of a census (Luke 2). Why would a government bother with a census if not to have some instrument for measuring change and dealing with it?

The Christian faith might not have experienced growth from "Jerusalem . . . to the end of the earth" if change were not already sweeping the world of that day. Passage through the empire by sea and land were safe because Roman legions guaranteed the protection of commerce. At the same time, the large slave population was restless. Not only was change continuous in the New Testament period, but *revolutionary* change was always just around the corner. The Christian faith was ideally suited for such a transitional period of history. The gospel meant a new breakthrough to a people living in a period eagerly looking for change.

Certainly the New Testament book of Acts testifies to a community of persons who combined an effective set of values and purposes with a readiness to try anything and go anywhere. Was this daring pioneer spirit unrelated to their strong Christian conviction? Or were they ready to venture into the unknown precisely because they did have a faith that eagerly anticipated the future, that considered change as evidence of God's activity in human history?

2 *THE LORD OF CHANGE*

MANY CHRISTIANS DEPLORE today's revolutionary changes. They assume that the way things have been is the way they should be, and therefore they sincerely insist that stability, tranquility, and order are God's intention for mankind. It may come as a shock for such people to discover that God frequently works through revolutions, both the peaceful variety and the violent kind. The witness of both the Old and New Testaments is quite clear that revolutionary changes in society and history are often the intention of God.

The Bible speaks to the issues generated by change. As we read it, we discover how men and women of faith have seen God active through change and have responded to the challenges which the great shifts of history have posed. Through their experience we can gain help in dealing constructively with the new situations brought about by present-day change.

To the Old Testament prophets God was the changer of history, the one who would overturn the old order to bring about a new one if necessary. Man lived constantly under God's immediate control. Such a God could and would take any necessary action to gain his purpose for mankind, and no change in the social structure was too radical, not even one which involved sacrificing his beloved nation,

Israel. The message of the prophets, therefore, was (as one Bible scholar has put it) "not evolutionist or reformist, but revolutionary." The same writer continues, "They were social revolutionaries because they were religious conservatives, seeking to revive the essential ethics and social creativity" of the historic faith.[1]

This powerful God could do whatever he deemed best. Unlike the pagan deities who were believed to live in some local grove of trees or a tall mountain, the God of Israel was not limited by the forces of nature. He could move powerfully, using history as the arena of his activity. By his intervention he could lead his people out of Egypt, giving a redemptive religious meaning to the political and historical event known as the Exodus.

Furthermore the God who set people free from bondage was a jealous God. This close relationship between his action in history and his jealousy is quite clearly seen in Exodus 20:2-5 and Deuteronomy 5:6-9: "I am the LORD your God, who brought you out of the land of Egypt, out of the house of bondage. You shall have no other gods before me . . . you shall not bow down to them or serve them; for I the LORD your God am a jealous God. . . ." This watchful concern of the all-powerful mover and changer of history, intolerant of any other gods (be they idols or idolatrous social systems), kept the loyal Hebrew worshiper critical of the society in which he lived. Thus the faithful Israelite was denied the seeming comfort of conformity to the social and economic status quo.

The Hebrew prophets recognized a tension between the *revealed* order (what God intends for man and nature) and the *actual* order (what man has been able to do with nature and history). As one writer put it:

A profound disharmony exists between the will of God and the existing social order. God in his redemptive work stands in judgment upon man for his sin, and the startling affirmation is made that man and his society can only be redeemed through the purifying fire of Divine judgment. The Israelite desired peace and harmony as deeply as any man, but he lived for the most part in a world of disharmony. Consequently, revolution was expected; even though feared, it was seen to be a necessity before the revealed order could be consummated.[2]

THE CONTRAST WITH ISRAEL'S NEIGHBORS

Contrast this point of view with the attitudes of Israel's pagan neighbors, whose religious systems exalted the status quo. Many of these cults were nature and fertility religions, which were chiefly concerned with making certain that the natural processes of rain, sun, and fruitful earth would continue in their regular cycle. Droughts and floods were believed to be evidences that the gods were displeased because the status quo had been disturbed in some way. Therefore the members of these fertility cults felt that they had to try desperately to maintain the existing social order in order to assure the deities of their loyalty.

This tendency to maintain *what already is* worked out in an interesting fashion in Egypt, where the king was regarded as a god and therefore was supposed to be immortal. The preservation of the body in the form of a mummy and its interment in a great pyramid as a residence for eternity are evidence of this extravagant concern for longevity. Persons of lesser rank believed that their chances for immortality depended on their degree of favor with the Pharaoh and their physical nearness to him. Therefore they made great efforts to be buried near the dead king whom they had served. Their good deeds in his behalf were recorded by inscriptions on the wall to remind him what loyal and helpful servants they had been. It is readily apparent that in such a social system, where immortality depended on the favor of the king, an attitude of submissiveness was guaranteed.

Canaan is another ancient land where we can easily see the sharp contrast between the worship of one God by the Hebrews and of many gods, or baals, by the Canaanites. Imagine the change that took place in the life of an Israelite when he arrived in Canaan. He had been living as a nomadic shepherd in the desert, as his fathers had lived for generations before him. Now, as he began to settle down to farming in his new land, who would normally assist him in learning how to live? Obviously, the neighboring farmers, who were Canaanites, worshipers of the "lords" or "baals" of the fields. Like the Pilgrims in colonial New England, who learned from the Indians how to plant corn in a mound of soil with five grains of seed and a fish for fertilizer, the Israelites were guided by the agricultural practices of the Canaanites. When he asked his Canaanite neighbor, "What's best to plant around here?" the neighbor's reply would include some advice about the rites of homage to the lord of the field, the baal. Consequently the Israelite, like the local farmers, would be tempted to go to some hill or lone tree, or perhaps to a grove of trees, where the local baal was supposed to live, and ask him to bless the crop.

An Old Testament scholar interprets this Canaanite practice: "Baal ensured fertility of the soil and thus guaranteed self-preservation. . . .

To secure fertility one must therefore satisfy the pleasure of the Baal. He naturally withheld his gifts to those who refused . . . him his due." [3]

Thus the word was out among all of Israel's neighbors, from Egypt to Assyria to Canaan: "Keep the gods happy; don't rock the boat." Against this vast array of cosmic and natural forces which were massed to defend the status quo, the loyal Israelite was called to stand ready at any moment for revolutionary change. This he did because he knew his God to be active in history. He knew also that his God was a jealous God, jealous of his place as creator and redeemer. The Hebrew was made aware that God judges "what is" by what God, himself, reveals to be his divine intent for mankind. [4]

GOD WORKS THROUGH HISTORY

For the Israelite, therefore, it was neither nature nor the universe but the history of human events itself that came to have profound meaning. Because he understood that the dynamic will of God can be revealed within history, the Hebrew was not frozen within a rigid social apparatus. Thus he escaped the servile role which was allotted to the pagan. He accepted the responsibility of interpreting God's will and helping to bring about its realization, however much this might clash with the political authority of his day.

This unique relationship of God to the Hebrew people is clearly seen in the boldness of the prophet Nathan as he confronted his king, the powerful David, with the dastardly character of David's crime in ordering the murder of Bathsheba's soldier-husband. You recall the scene. A country preacher comes into the royal court and approaches the great king. The king listens to a seemingly irrelevant story of a wealthy man who provides for his table by stealing a neighbor family's pet ewe. The plain injustice of such a greedy action angers the king. Then, with the words, "You are the man!" Nathan breaks through and exposes the guilt which has been hidden in King David's heart.

Would any other ruler of that day have confessed as David did, "I have sinned against the Lord"? Indeed, would a commoner have been given a hearing by any other oriental monarch? Because God alone is Lord, the King of Israel was, in the final analysis, restrained from being a despot.

Another prophet who showed a deep awareness of God's revolutionary intervention in national affairs was Amos of Tekoa. This outspoken shepherd delivered his prophetic words to a people most reluctant to listen—pilgrims who had returned to a hallowed religious place and were in no mood to hear the awful word of their unfaithfulness which he pronounced. We can understand their attitude. Were they not at Bethel to honor God? The fact that they had journeyed long distances to make this religious pilgrimage spoke for itself, did it not? Besides, didn't the very prosperity of Israel and Judah reflect God's favor upon the two great kings who ruled them? When had there been such an expanding economy? When had the people ever felt so secure and comfortable? When had the armies been so victorious?

It was this very attitude of "We've never had it so good!" that hid from Israel her real condition. Amos pointed to the putrid sore that lay behind the façade of prosperity as he thundered the word of the Lord: "After crime upon crime of Israel I will not relent, for they sell honest folk for money, the needy for a pair of shoes, they trample down the poor like dust . . ." (Amos 2:6, 7, Moffatt). Amos reminded Israel that it has always been God who started the action: "Yet it was I who brought you up from Egypt's land; for forty years I led you through the desert . . ." (Amos 2:10, Moffatt). In a few words he described the evil for which the nation has been condemned: "For they do not know how to do right, who treasure up violence and robbery in their palaces" (Amos 3:10, Smith and Goodspeed).

Behind Amos' words is his awareness of a major social problem. The military defeat of Damascus by Jereboam II had allowed Israel to control the trade routes of Damascus and Arabia. While this created a class of wealthy traders, it also sharpened the differences between rich and poor. The great wealth enjoyed by Israel's elite is evident in the prophet's promise that God would cause the destruction of "both winter house and summer house." We can feel the acid sting of the prophet's words if we think "Suburbia" instead of "Samaria" as the prophet denounces society's leading ladies (Amos 4:1, Moffatt): "Listen to this, you cows of Bashan, you women in high Samaria, you who defraud the poor and are hard on the needy, who tell your husbands, 'Let us have wine to drink!'" (In the mid-sixties, slick-paper magazine advertisements for an expensive whiskey showed a well-dressed matron saying to her husband, "While you're up, get me a. . . .") Amos' pronouncements are not far from the headlines seen frequently in our metropolitan daily newspapers: "I know your countless crimes, your manifold misdeeds—browbeating honest men, accepting bribes, defrauding the poor of justice" (Amos 5:12, Moffatt).

WHY DO WE IGNORE THE PROPHET?

Perhaps one reason we fail to sense the prophet's rebuke as a judgment upon our own times is that we have idealized so much of the prophetic message. For example, consider what comes to mind when you hear these words (Isaiah 30:15, Smith and Goodspeed):

> "By returning and resting shall you be saved,
> In quietness and confidence shall be your strength."

Do you think in religious terms, imagining a place of spiritual retreat or perhaps a quiet sanctuary for meditation? Or do you recognize that these words were uttered in a time of political crisis as the prophet's plan for his nation's conduct of her international affairs? Martin Buber has pointed out that Isaiah was proposing a reliable political program for the Israelites living in Canaan.[5] He was calling the nation from her reliance upon superior weapons and military alliances and urging, instead, a return to trusting God as the judge of history, for God is sovereign over all human enterprises.

The widely held assumption that God was concerned only with Israel's immediate interests led to a major oversight on Israel's part. Many of the people thought of God as a high-class "baal" or god of the fatherland, and not as the God of all the earth. This misconception was popular not only among the rank-and-file but among the religious leaders as well. While on the one hand they talked about the worldwide sovereignty of God, on the other they prided themselves as select in his sight, thus turning the awesome greatness of God into a national asset. In this respect Israel was not unlike many modern nations who try to reduce the LORD God to a national deity in order to evade his divine demands of justice and equity for all men.

By idealizing a Bible text we minimize its demands upon us in our present situation. Consider for instance, Isaiah 1:18:

> . . . though your sins are like scarlet,
> they shall be as white as snow;
> though they are red like crimson,
> they shall become like wool.

What does "sins" mean here? Many of us will answer only in terms of personal actions and moral habits, but sins can also involve social responsibility and ethical practicality. Which does this great verse of divine forgiveness have to do with? Turn to Isaiah 1:17 and let the prophet answer for himself:

> . . . learn to do good;
> seek justice,
>   correct oppression;
> defend the fatherless,
>   plead for the widow.

The two verses, taken together, define an important element in the true believer's relation to God. Learn, says the prophet, as you have not yet learned, what God requires as your service. With the same devotion with which you seek God in worship, so seek justice. The dimension of social responsibility is essential to true worship. In making this emphasis, the prophet spells out the distinctive characteristic of Hebrew worship, namely that God alone is sovereign and that he maintains a strict watch over his domain. This watchful care is symbolized by his compassion for the orphan and the widow. Such a God, in his demand for justice, can also demand the upset of those who block his purposes.

GOD'S WILL THREATENS SOCIAL AND POLITICAL STATUS

As the men who gave voice to this understanding, the prophets gained a reputation for turning over the standing order (see 1 Kings 11:29-39 and 2 Kings 9:4-13, for example). The tradition of Hebrew prophecy is essentially an engagement with history. Where the pagan religions would blame fate or the whimsy of capricious deities as the cause of radical social change, the Hebrew prophets saw social upheaval as a way in which God brought about the divine government of right and justice.

The prophets reminded Israel, caught in the tortuous snarl of historical change, that it is God himself who acts, and not some unknown deity or fickle fate. Jeremiah, for instance, told of God's divine purpose first to pull out by the roots and "to break down, to destroy and to overthrow," and then "to build and to plant" (Jeremiah 1:10). Destruction was to give way to new creation, according to Jeremiah's call.

The consistent witness of both Old and New Testaments is that God is the LORD of change. The connecting link between the two covenants is the figure of the servant. This is obvious in the Magnificat, which reads almost like a revolutionary manifesto (Luke 1:52-53, N.E.B.):

> "He has torn imperial powers from their thrones,
>   but the humble have been lifted high.
> The hungry he has satisfied with good things,
>   the rich sent empty away."

How well these words apply to the twentieth century! The nineteen-hundreds opened with Germany, England, and France extending their worldwide empires, even as Spain's last outposts were slipping away. Now today, with a third of our century still to go, we have watched these vast empires fade away as new, young nations emerge. Is there a connection between the missionary movement that went out to set souls free and today's movements to set societies free? The noted economist Barbara Ward thinks so. She says:

> . . . perhaps the sharpest break in Western tradition from the basic ideas of other civilizations lies in its vision of reality as an unfolding drama, as an immense dialogue between God and man. . . .[6]

JESUS INTERPRETS GOD'S PLAN

As Israel was led by the prophets to listen to God's calling, the responsibility more and more took on the character of a servant ministry. Certainly it was the figure of the suffering servant that gave to Jesus' ministry its unique quality.[7]

Servanthood is the decisive response of man to God's command. The servant may be called to exercise judgment, to establish peace, and even to set the commonwealth aright. When Jesus came to his home synagogue and was called upon to read, an honor graciously extended to a native son now a distinguished rabbi, he chose words from the prophet Isaiah which expressed this idea (Luke 4:18-19):

> "The Spirit of the Lord is upon me,
> because he has anointed me to preach good news to the poor.
> He has sent me to proclaim release to the captives
> and recovering of sight to the blind,
> to set at liberty those who are oppressed,
> to proclaim the acceptable year of the Lord."

His own comments which followed the reading were intended to allow the congregation to recognize him as Isaiah's prophet-servant.

Jesus was alerting his countrymen to God's kingdom which was breaking in upon them, but the people of Nazareth rejected his message and thus his mission. Jesus was not downcast by rejection, however; instead he saw himself as the cornerstone of a new Israel (Luke 20:17). A similar meaning is expressed in the parable of the vine-growers, where the owner of the vineyard exercises his sovereignty despite his rebellious tenants. Jesus declared that God would use violent change if necessary in order to establish his rule (Luke 20: 9-18).

We have seen how the Bible testifies, from Moses to Isaiah to Jesus, that Israel's faith is a revolutionary one. Men and women weaned on the Hebrew-Christian heritage are not afraid to upset the existing social and political patterns when necessary. Such a faith has contributed to western civilization a readiness for drastic change in the standing order. Men of faith have sensed God's breaking-through the man-made crust of history in events like the Reformation, the signing of the Magna Charta, and the Declaration of Independence.

This does not imply that God is necessarily in every revolution. As H. H. Rowley has said, "Nowhere in the Bible is it taught that all history is the revelation of God, or that everything that happens reflects His will." [8] We are only to understand that there is always the *possibility* that God is using current revolutions to bring about his divine rule of equity, justice, and peace. We dare not ignore such revolutions or automatically reject them, for there is always the possibility that through them he is doing what man will not let him do in any other way.

THE BIBLE AS RESOURCE FOR LIFE

Christians have a wonderfully valuable resource in the Bible. It can help them face change, even change of revolutionary proportions. To harness such assistance, however, they need to learn how to listen to its prophetic voice. Therefore the church's teaching ministry must prepare persons to respond creatively to situations of change. It must offer a dynamic concept for studying the Bible, in which there is opportunity to learn through experience. The gospel and contemporary life must be closely related if Christians are to live creatively among the convulsive problems of today. Intense Bible study may precede responsible involvement in contemporary social problems, or it may follow such involvement when a person is driven to study the Bible because his action in the midst of life has raised unanswered concerns.

We seem to approach the Bible with mixed feelings. On the one hand, we cherish it. The Bible remains a best seller, and no home is considered complete without one or more copies. Equally obvious, on the other hand, however, is our ignorance of the Bible's contents and meaning. Even though we buy it in ever so many bindings and translations, we don't seem to read it with understanding—if, indeed, we read it at all.

If the growing Christian is to appreciate God's lordship over change, he needs to engage in a dynamic kind of Bible study. He needs to move beyond a routine of ten verses a day to a serious reading of the letters, poetry, and books that together provide the Bible's view of life. He needs to understand what the writers of the various books of the Bible meant to communicate in their day and what this means now. It is important to approach the Bible with an awareness that it can speak to our present condition and that our own day-to-day experiences in turn can illuminate many of its meanings. We need to study the Bible in terms of life as we are experiencing it. This is extremely important, but in itself it is not enough. We must not limit the Bible to the small space our experiences have hollowed out; rather we may broaden our lives as we discover new meanings in our Bible study.

Serious Bible study should lead us to see the Bible as a whole—and to see life as the Bible writers saw it. It is important to "think biblically" because the Bible's God-centered philosophy of life has been worked out in the real events of human endeavors.

One of the principal advantages of the new materials for church school teaching currently being developed by Protestant denominations is that the Bible is central and is used in relation to the life of the learner. More will be said on this subject in the discussion of the crossing point (Chapter 5), but first let us observe how the planners themselves have stated it:

> As the library of revelation, the Bible is not only a record of how God revealed himself in the past and how man has responded in the past, it is also a present instrument of revelation for any who are enabled to see themselves as part of the historical community addressed by God. For many who seek him, "God's word to man" as revealed in the Bible has exhibited the power to become "God's word to me." Because of this power the Christian Scriptures are given a central and unique position in the church's educational ministry.[9]

If the Christian gospel is to influence the whole life span of individuals, we must recognize that as increasing numbers of our young people go on to the colleges and universities they will be working daily with "the scientific approach." In fact, many of them will encounter it in the public schools long before they go to college. Therefore, in our earliest teaching of the Bible, we must avail ourselves of the insights of those Bible scholars who have drawn on the findings of such sciences as philology, archeology, and anthropology. Such an awareness of the "scientific approach" on the part of teachers can help a generation of Christians to avoid the false traps of those followers of scientism who claim to be "purely objective," yet who are actually biased against religion.

Above all, the Bible must be studied in relation to life. If God is to be recognized as Lord over history, he must be met in the changes taking place around us. Even as we study the Bible with the aid of theologians and archeologists, we must also seek him within the social movements of our time. For example, one group of Bible students inquired: "Is God always and only revolutionary?" They also asked, "What does revolution mean?" At the time this group was meeting to think and talk together, major American cities were erupting with riots in the streets. This led to further questions: "How can we determine what God is doing?" "Is it possible for God to work through riots?" "Does God punish?" "When is a demonstration Christian and when is it non-Christian?"

Although it is possible to go directly to the Bible for answers, this is not always the most helpful thing to do first. Sometimes we have to become involved personally in an issue before we can understand what the Bible is saying about it. Think, for instance, about the question, "Does God punish?" When Jesus was faced with the same inquiry, he answered with a question of his own: "What about those eighteen in Siloam who were killed when the tower fell on them? Do you suppose this proves that they were worse than all the other people living in Jerusalem?" Jesus' answer to his own question can be found by reading Luke 13:5: "I tell you, No; but unless you repent you will all likewise perish."

Bible study is not enough unless it is coupled with redemptive action among people who are personally experiencing the sores and abrasions of life. Depth Bible study, the kind that really matters, is more than just philosophical, theoretical, or mental gymnastics. It requires that students be part of the action, seeking to discover where God is at work in contemporary change to learn whether they are aiding or thwarting his purposes. To appreciate fully the plight of the disinherited of this earth requires that we share in first-hand acquaintance of actual conditions. Certainly, Jesus did just this.

The opportunities to learn through experience will vary from situation to situation, taking into account the age and experience level of the learner as well as the teacher. Field trips, work projects, leisure-time experiences (such as day camping and nature hikes), and service projects all provide clues as to how meaningful experiences of learning through activity might be planned and provided.

Here is how one planned-for learning experience uncovered another which was less structured but no less meaningful. Returning from a visit to Mariners' Temple on Manhattan's lower east side, a college group walked across town on the narrow tip of the island. The leader of the group pointed to a towering bank building which stood tall and bright against the night sky. One of the co-eds exclaimed, "Oh, that is the building Mother and I picketed." The girl had previously accompanied her mother in a protest demonstration which was related to a social issue involving financial investments in South Africa.

Christian insights can come at some of the seemingly most unlikely times and places. If this girl has come from a home where the Bible is known as a living book and if her church provides a program of Christian education where God is known and taught as one who is active in human affairs, then this young person's faith may find lasting meaning in picketing. She has had the opportunity to learn through this activity that God is sovereign over all of history and that God does work redemptively through social change. And, furthermore, those who discussed the incident with her on the glittering city streets of Manhattan at night have had the opportunity to share in her discovery.

3 MISSION AMIDST REVOLUTION

REVOLUTION IS THE KEY WORD to modern history. Revolutionary change is taking place, not only within Christianity but in almost every area of present-day life. Radical changes are occurring in the social order, in civil rights, in technology and urbanization, among and within nations. "Revolutionary" describes the impact of modern medicine, electronics, and supersonics upon golden-agers and college students alike.

The church too is undergoing great change. "This steady and peaceful revolution" were the words chosen by a Roman Catholic prelate to describe the vast transitions taking place within his church. He stressed that change was essential if Christians were to carry the gospel to modern men, and his words have been no less appropriate to Protestants than to his own church.

As some persons consider the current revolution, they wonder. For instance, a member of a minority whose legal rights and social opportunities have been withheld for over a hundred years might well ask: "How steady is this revolution?" A person whose job has been wiped out by the new technology or whose business has been gutted by street riots might ask: "How peaceful is this revolution?" But no man or woman sensitive to the magnitude of the changes taking place in our lifetimes will deny that the word "revolutionary" properly describes our situation.

A replay of some recent history may alert us to the real danger in the Christian church when it fails to recognize the possibility that God uses revolt to fashion history. Father Adolfs, the Augustinian Prior at Eindhoven, The Netherlands, has described the inadequate role played by his church in the social changes of the nineteenth and twentieth centuries. Though this analysis deals with the Roman Catholic church, it fits the general pattern followed by Protestant churches in Europe, England, and the United States during the same period.

Father Adolfs writes of the coming of the industrial revolution and with it the rise of an economy based upon capital investment. This places an unbearable burden onto the landless and moneyless lower class. As every reader of Charles Dickens knows, England early experienced the tragic brunt of the new industrial age. The immensity of the problem is evident in these comparative figures: In 1840, for instance, a Liverpool working man could expect to live fifteen years of a hard life, whereas the average life expectancy for a person of his age was thirty-five years. In 1863 a concerned member of Parliament tried to arouse the social conscience of his colleagues with the shocking fact that, though the cotton industry was only ninety years old, in its three generations of existence in England it had used up nine generations of workers!

How did the church respond to the crying need for reform? Its predominant voice seems to have counseled only "contentedness." Wait for heaven's rewards, and for the present be content with the charitable inclinations of the mill owners. Father Adolfs quotes the Dutch periodical *De Katholiek* for 1880:

> The social question springs from a political conspiracy. The solution to the prevailing unrest lies in *contentedness,* the contented spirit with which the working people must bear their lot, because they are Christians. The last word on the social question is the kindly disposition of the better sort of persons and the charity which their love disposes them to exercise.[1]

Though churchmen, along with the ruling classes, were indifferent to this condition of abject poverty, the communist pioneer Karl Marx directed his bitter writings against the problem.

Father Adolfs also describes the communist takeover in Hungary and shows how the church was tied to the backward economy in that country. Until World War II sixty-seven percent of the Hungarian population were Roman Catholic, and their church was the largest single landholder. Yet in this same country existed two and a half million peasants without land and living in poverty. Not until 1943 did any religious group make a move to change the situation, namely the Cistercians, who divided about five thousand hectares (twelve thousand acres) of their land among the peasants living on it. But this was too little and too late. Father Adolfs writes: "When at last the Russians came, agrarian reform was put through, by main force, within a matter of days." [3] Again it was the communists who responded where the Christians had failed. We may recall that many centuries ago it was another "outside" nation, that of the Persians, which God used for his divine purposes (see Isaiah 45:1ff).

Sensitivity to the need for change often comes from unexpected sources. In our century there have been a number of bearded and bathless protest movements against the status quo, of which the beatnik and the hippie have been two expressions. One might well ask why this revulsion against "the great mother bar soap." Do the protests of these people contain an element of the prophetic? Is their refusal to go along with the deodorized and sanitized world around them anything like Jesus' scorching indictment of the social leaders of his time? "You clean the outside of cup and plate; but inside you there is nothing but greed and wickedness" (Luke 11:39, N.E.B.). One does not have to approve of all the immature conduct of the beard-and-sandal cult to recognize the validity of some of their judgments. Some observers have seen a similarity in their dress and denunciation to that of the great prophet John the Baptist, who declared: ". . . the axe is laid to the root of the trees. . . ." Radical (that is, "to the very roots") changes are occurring and will occur, in every nation on the earth—some for social or political reasons, others because of technological advance.

In an entirely different way our families are feeling the pressures of our changing world. A mother who had lived in one community from birth until college was concerned for the welfare of her children. As the wife of a rapidly advancing corporation executive, she felt that they were not experiencing the stable kind of childhood she herself had known. Because of Dad's many transfers, their oldest son was now enrolled in his sixth high school in three years. For this woman there was at least a partial answer. When she shared her concern with a friend, the friend said, "Even a family on the move can know God and the values of love, home life, and the service of others." Since both were familiar with the Scriptures, they talked together about Israel's pilgrimage. "Look at the years of training for Israel as the people wandered for forty years. A nation on the move developed a deep appreciation for God's guidance. Can it happen to a modern family?" Although the conversation did not resolve the mother's immediate concern, her friend's remarks did enable her to examine her situation from a new perspective.

Still another aspect of the problem is found in the vocational scene. Automation forced a man, in his early fifties, out of his supervisory job. It was the only work he had ever done. Other men in the same predicament took to loafing around the pool halls and bars. This man, however, though numbed by the sudden loss of what everybody had assumed was a lifetime position, sensed that "loafing around" would not help his personality and outlook. He tried to find employment in the kind of work he knew best. When this effort failed, he stopped to consider, "What have I always wanted to do?" In his case, he had a great interest in the work of the church. He offered his services to an area office of his denomination. Soon he was taking university courses while serving some small congregations in a leadership role. A new career and life of service thus opened to the man who was not afraid to face the consequences of change.

AREAS OF CHANGE

The flood tide of revolutionary change which characterizes our times can be seen more clearly if we contrast certain marks of the nineteenth century with those of the twentieth:

Nineteenth Century	*Twentieth Century*
Individual	Corporate
Private	Public
Personal	Social
Religious	Secular

The first of these changes from *individual* to *corporate,* can be seen in the personalities of some of the prominent figures in American society of the nineteenth and twentieth centuries. We can compare the writings of such men as Ralph Waldo Emerson and Russell Conwell with twentieth-century personalities like Martin Luther King, Jr. and even President Johnson's Defense Secretary, Robert McNamara. Whereas Emerson and Conwell were individualists, the strength of

King and McNamara has been in their ability to deal with diverse movements and highly complex organizations.

The nineteenth century produced great movements, to be sure, such as the great missionary societies and the abolitionist movement, but persons identified themselves with these primarily on a voluntary basis. The twentieth-century movements, on the other hand, take the form of blocs—groupings of peoples more formally organized, like the great labor unions or the American Medical Association. Neither of these depends on voluntary support, certainly not the "free association" of the nineteenth-century movements, for each has fixed obligations for its members. A person almost automatically joins the labor organization or the medical association because of his job or profession. Similarly, in the nineteenth century, scientific advance and technological change were usually the products of individual labors, as for example, the inventions of Thomas Edison, Alexander Graham Bell, or the Wright brothers, whereas twentieth-century research and development can be "big" science with tens and hundreds of men engaged in a single research project.

The accent on the corporate does not eliminate the need for the individual. To understand his new role, he must recognize the tendency of modern corporate society to deny his identity, but he must also see that corporate structure does not require conformity. To appreciate the true meaning of the corporate, Christians must recover an understanding of the biblical idea of the covenant—the individual person as an essential part of a community. Such covenantal theology has a significant role for the responsible person today, for the contemporary community requires the commitment of the participating individual.

The trend from *private* to *public* is another way of illustrating a similar development. One hundred years ago most business and manufacturing firms were family owned and operated, with the father and son daily involved in the enterprise. Today, however, business and industry are dominated by corporations owned by the public through stockholding. Likewise the individually owned grocery store, where the grocer's family lived upstairs, is being replaced by the chain supermarket. We have also witnessed the increasing participation of government in fields formerly occupied only by private enterprise.

In light of these transitions it is not surprising to find that the *personal* has also been yielding to the *social*. Our grandfathers may have been hired directly by the owner of the small mill, but the procedure is more complicated today. We go to an employment office for an interview with a personnel director, who guides us through a maze of applications, evaluations, and procedures. The once-simple employer-employee relationship has developed into "industrial relations," with complex negotiations between representatives of management and the labor unions. We recognize these developments as inevitable results of the growth of our national economy.

In a similar vein, we increasingly expect organizations to solve our personal problems for us. When a small group of college students went to a sympathetic member of the state legislature with the request for certain legislation in their behalf, the legislator had one recommendation. "Go back," he said, "to your campus and organize. Then send your representatives down here to lobby for students. We don't listen to individuals; we pay attention to organized groups."

The first three changes we have been discussing are closely related. Less direct is the connection of these with the equally significant shift from the apparently *religious* tone of the nineteenth century to the largely *secular* temper of the twentieth. The connection is there, however. For example, American higher education has been moving away from the private college, which provided quality education for a few, toward the public university, which attempts to educate the many. Church-related colleges, which dominated higher education in the 1800's are now giving way to the vastly larger, less selective universities of the late 1900's. The motivation for the denominationally founded liberal arts college was good. It was to provide leadership for religion and society. The motivation for public universities is also good, but it is different from the earlier schools. The university strives to provide leaders for business, industry, government, etc. Thus the religious motivation for college education has been displaced by the secular effort to provide leadership for the expanding society.

The secularization of society is not necessarily all bad. Much of nineteenth-century individualism did not really allow for the development of the individual. In contrast, today we are in one of the most optimistic periods of history ever offered to the Christian church. Secular society provides the possibility for men and women to become authentically human individuals. The challenge to Christians is to demonstrate a style of life that fits into this new situation.

Let us not hide the fact, however, that there is a difference of opinion on this important matter. The debate is illustrated by two British intellectuals, both of whom write from a Christian perspective but who take opposite views on whether society should be sacred or secular in its orientation. One of these is T. S. Eliot, noted American-born British poet, who in his essay "The Idea of a Christian Society" makes an eloquent case for a social order based upon explicitly Christian values. He calls for a new concept of Christendom as located wherever man's social existence is built upon laws and customs consciously derived from Christian roots:

> It is only in a society with a religious basis—which is not the same thing as an ecclesiastical despotism—that you can get the proper harmony and tension, for the individual or for the community.
> . . . The Community of Christians is not an organization, but a body of indefinite outline; composed of both clergy and laity, of the more conscious, more spiritually and intellectually developed of both. It will be their identity of belief and aspiration, their background of a common system of education and a common culture, which will enable them to influence and be influenced by each other, and collectively to form the conscious mind and the conscience of the nation.[3]

Denys Munby takes the opposite position in *The Idea of a Secular Society.* He defines a secular society as "one which explicitly refuses to commit itself as a whole to any particular view of the nature of the universe and the place of man in it." Such a society, he explains, is in practice pluralistic, that is, made up of many different kinds of persons who confess many different traditions and express varying and perhaps conflicting understandings in regard to life. The secular society, Munby adds, is also tolerant in that it "gives every benefit of doubt to the varied expression of belief" and is ready to take risks to allow for wide differences.[4] He contends that the secular society accords with Christian purposes because it allows man greater freedom to develop than has ever been possible where governments have been dominated by the church or even by a religious point of view.[5]

What do such writers mean when they use the word "secular"? It comes to us from the distinction drawn between the "religious" and the "secular" priests in the Middle Ages. Those in the monasteries were "religious" because they belonged to religious orders, whereas the ordinary parish cleric who lived out in the world was the secular priest. Today, some people associate the word "secular" with vice and "religious" with virtue, but "secular" should be relieved of this stigma, for historically it means no more than "in the world." Actually, if the Protestant ministry, particularly the ministry of the laity, has any rootage in history at all, its rootage is in the *secular* priesthood of the Middle Ages.

The casual reader might imagine that the changes described in these pages could be summarized in the shift from an urban to a rural culture. Such is not the case, however. Would that it were so simple! Actually, the rural is experiencing just as radical a change as the urban. What, then, are the characteristics that presently affect both rural and urban communities?

The Former	*The Present*
static	dynamic
homogeneous	pluralistic
settled	mobile
traditional	innovative

Whereas former generations lived in a largely *static* situation, the people of today all around the world face a *dynamic* situation. There are political, economic, social, technological, and other reasons for this change. Communities and even regions which once were largely *homogeneous,* with similar cultures and shared thought patterns, today increasingly are composed of *pluralistic* groups, including minorities of significant size and influence. Where once we were a *settled* people, our families are increasingly *mobile.* Our young people tend to migrate. When people retire, more and more they tend to move to new homes, often in more comfortable climates. For many reasons our society, once dominated by *tradition,* is now increasingly influenced by *innovation.* Whereas once we argued our case from precedent, "It's always been done this way," we now tend to argue from the novel, "It has never been tried this way before." That it has never been done before has an enormous appeal and is effective and persuasive.

THEOLOGY EXPOSED TO CHANGE

In this time when Christians are being called to take the changing secular world more seriously as the arena for God's reconciling action, churchmen are discovering theology itself to be in a state of near-explosive ferment. In our own decade the problem is freshly stated in new, or renewed, controversies. One of these controversies has to do with "the new morality." This attempt to develop new moral understandings arises out of a renewed awareness of the perplexities of modern ethical situations accompanied by a frustration with the rigid death-mask character of much of traditional morality. Some of the names that come to mind are those of Episcopalians James Pike and Joseph F. Fletcher and Baptist Howard Moody,* who hold that the new morality seeks to express the liberty found in Jesus Christ. The move among such modern-day critics is toward responsible freedom as a replacement for moral laws and regulations. In their own way they are attempting, like Jesus, to cleanse traditional religion of its Pharisaism. Critics of this position hold that these men have let the pigeons and goats loose in the temple but have not been able to sweep them out. They say that too many persons miss the point and mistake liberty to mean license, so that the "new morality" becomes no morality.

A second strand of controversy comes from the "secular" theologians, men like Colin Williams, Harvey Cox, and Denys Munby, who are trying to ease Christians out of what they consider the prison house of "religion" into the open air of God's world, the secular arena.[7] The typical Christian must be as confused as was the synagogue goer in the days when Jesus was accusing the leading churchmen of his day, the Pharisees, of betraying God's purposes.

Some writers feel that Cox has overstated his case, for to them he seems to suggest that all that is religious is bad and all that is secular is good. John Bennett, among others, has inserted a note of caution at this point. He affirms Cox's position in part, but then goes on to add a warning:

> Christians have good reason to celebrate the secular, especially when it gives some promise of taking the form of a healthy pluralism, of free competition between human systems. . . . However, I am disturbed by the tendency to celebrate the secular in such a way as to allow too much that goes under this name to remain without Christian criticism.[8]

Such writers as Cox and Munby have made us aware of the elements within modern secular culture that seem to fit in with God's ultimate purpose for mankind. It is possible for such elements to help free modern man from tribal tyrannies, ideologies which oppress, and prejudices that limit. Nevertheless, as Bennett makes plain, we cannot say that *all* secular forces are beneficial, for many of them lack the high liberating quality of secularism at its best. In fact there are forces within our secular civilization that would deny any man his God-given dignity. Bennett has reminded us that Dietrich Bonhoeffer, whose phrase "the world come of age" provided a starting point for much of the current acclaim of the secular, was himself done to death by such a force. We are not yet free of those demonic "principalities and powers" that continue to divide people and to make persons less than they are.

In the present rise of secularism we must maintain a perspective that allows for judgment. Let us pray that the church will be alert and will take its part in whatever good things are emerging. At the same time the church must remain independent enough of the world to call into question the evil and injustice in it. Jesus, in his parable of the wheat and the tares, recognized the problem of discerning God's action within human history. We can appreciate that writers like Cox and Munby have helped us to see some of God's wheat in the secular field that we so long thought was sown only with tares. Christians need to go into the fields to work with all sorts and conditions of men in order to prepare for the harvest God intends, for the good of all mankind.

A third strand of controversy comes through the so-called radical theologians such as William Hamilton, Thomas J. Altizer, and Paul Van Buren, who first became known to many through the phrase "the death of God." Their views cannot be dismissed lightly, for they are criticizing the idea of an eternal omnipotent being who exists apart from the natural world and only occasionally makes himself known through supernatural acts. Such a deity is not the God of Abraham, Moses, and Jesus. The living God is presence in love, coming to man in the person of Jesus to deliver man from that which limits. Love in Christ sets man free to be truly human, liberates him, and allows him to reach his potential selfhood.

Alienation causes contemporary man to feel that he has no personal experience of God today. This problem may be at the root of Hamilton's concern. Furthermore, the almost flippant manner in which Christians (both the run-of-the-mill variety and the deeply committed) idly drop the awesome name of God arouses rightly the reaction against "god language" in people such as Van Buren. Altizer seems to feel that modern technological man is not deeply moved by traditional Christian teachings and that some new and more powerful vehicle is necessary if his life is to be significantly affected. What may well trouble us in all these viewpoints is the assumption, or so it seems, that we modern men have powers of knowledge not available to ancient minds. Unfortunately, the success of technology allows modern man the vain luxury of imagining himself to be self-sufficient. But is he, really?

The Christian community is called to a definite mission and ministry in the midst of changes we have been considering. Christians are to seize the opportunity and make the best possible use of the new situation. In spite of the changes occurring in our world, the opportunity for effective exercise of a personal and social faith has by no means disappeared. In fact, if men use their intelligence and open themselves to spiritual powers, the twentieth century may prove to be more open to God's purposes than the nineteenth. This is where Christian education comes in. It asks questions like these:

—How do we maintain the individual within the corporate?

—How do we sustain the personal within the social?

—How do we enable the private to function within the public?

—How do we make the religious contribution within the secular?

The Christian as educator has an opportunity to affirm the value of the individual, private, and personal aspects of life, even in the midst of the corporate, public, and social setting. Thus we speak of a new arena for Christian education. The new situation created by rapid social change means that the church's ministry of teaching must go on today in a new and different frame of reference. The Christian community has a mission to help people face the demands of an increasingly secular order. To offer such help it must be a witnessing community, and the Christian educator who is truly concerned about education for change will quickly see that he is an essential element in such witness.

4   *SHAPERS OF CHANGE*

SOMEWHERE ALONG THE PILGRIMAGE called life, a child recognizes a self that is his own. The adults who have played major roles in his life may sense the dramatic discovery as the child who from birth has been called Karen now announces to all who will listen: "I am Lynn. My name is Lynn." They wonder what has happened.

By the time an individual recognizes his own unique being and begins to appreciate what it means to be a person, much of what he is has been determined for him. The pigmentation of his skin, his parents' station in life, his sex—all these conditioning factors and more—are not his to select, but they will push in upon him and affect his personal development. Whether we are born in America or Australia, we are all conditioned by influences such as geography, social custom, national traditions. In one country, for instance, people boast that their ancestors were among the first settlers; in another, there is status in being a more recent arrival. Again, we are influenced by whether we have been born into a closely knit family with congenial cousins and gracious grandparents or into a home broken by death or divorce. Even at the early age when we become aware of ourselves as persons, we still have much to learn about these conditioning factors and what they mean as we seek to answer the question "Who am I?"

Among college students, for example, it might be assumed that twelve years of schooling before college would allow ample opportunity for self-discovery. Yet frequently the freshman may try out a new name, and with it a new personality. The young lady we addressed for eighteen years as Jane is suddenly Mickey to her age-mates. She may even experiment with various new names suggesting a variety of personality styles. The girl who left home a brunette may return for her first holiday as a blonde, or the boy who went away with a brush-cut may come back in long hair and a beard.

This close relationship between one's name and one's expression of self may be seen in the Bible. Note how Abram becomes Abraham when he commits his life in response to God's invitation. Saul, the persecutor, is renamed Paul, who now becomes a different person as the great missioner.

GOD'S PLAN FOR MAN

One of the issues that persist throughout all of life is this question of self-identity. Despite a lot of talk that ours is a post-theological age, modern men continue to be seriously concerned with the theological question "Who is man?"

Two Scripture passages which aid us in understanding the nature of man are Psalm 8 and Genesis 1—3. In these he is seen as a creature fashioned in the likeness of his Creator and given responsibility for the use of all creation. Thus the Bible raises questions of man's social responsibility and the consequences of his living in relationship to others. It also opens questions involved in the application of science, questions of man's responsibility for his environment. It brings to our consciousness the issue of whether man is the victim or the author, or both, of sociological and technological change.

"What is man, that thou art mindful of him?" the psalmist asked, presupposing the relation of man to God. Samuel Terrien translates the next few lines this way:

> Yet Thou hast made him lack almost nothing divine,
> And hast crowned him with glory and honor.
> Thou hast given him rule over thy handiwork;
> Thou hast put all things under his feet. . . .[1]

Thus Psalm 8 sings the praise of the God who created the world for the sake of man. God has appointed man as his deputy, with the honor and responsibility for the supervision, maintenance, and use of this earthly endowment. Here is a hint of the tension between man's mortal condition and man as God's image, who has been given dominion over beasts and nature. Man is weak, like the beasts that perish (Psalm 49:12; 144:3). He is puny in comparison with the starlit heavens. Yet God has invested man with some of God's own dignity and has designated man as his representative on earth.

This intention of God for man is wonderfully spelled out in the stories of creation found in Genesis 1—3. God's power is made clear by the simple action with which, merely by his statement that *it is,* the created appears.[2] God creates all the heavens and the earth, the plants and the animals, without a second thought. But God then pauses to reflect and, after consideration, he brings man into being. Man is made in the image of God. As Alan Richardson observes, "This means that man shares with God the power of understanding truth, of creating what is beautiful and of doing what is right; in this man differs from every other living creature upon earth."[3]

It is important to recognize the emphasis of the Genesis accounts of creation. Bible scholars believe that these early narratives are more than just stories, for they communicate a never-exhausted truth regarding man's nature. Thus Genesis 1 in particular testifies to man's creatureliness under his Lord, and also to man's lordship over nature. God is the Creator, whereas man is part of God's creation with the responsibility of serving as steward or caretaker. God has given man the keys to creation.

Now, if man is made in God's image, why is man's life filled with so many problems—personal, domestic, social, and international? The ancient Hebrew wrestled with this question. Genesis 3 narrates the fall of Adam, who represents everyman. In man's desire to seize equality with his Creator, he rebels against God's will. This pride-filled rebellion is the essence of sin. Man confuses his own role with that of the Creator and refuses to fulfill God's purposes. Says J. A. Sanders: "Man's sin is his failure in some sense to distinguish between God and his blessings, the Giver and his gifts, the Creator and his creation."[4]

When we understand the significance of the Genesis stories, we are spared the supposed conflict between science and religion. Rather than debating the scientific pros and cons of these narratives, we center our attention on their theological message. Thus the fall of Adam describes a tragic dimension of human experience which is always present. It is a dramatic reminder that man continually repudiates the fellowship with God for which he has been created. Inevitably he rebels against his Creator.

How did Jesus understand the place of man in God's plan? Did Jesus see man as agent or captive of change? It is evident in the Gospels that Jesus, like the Old Testament prophets, saw God at work in the midst of life. At the same time he saw man as potential partner with God in the enterprise of human history. Profound change for the better is always a possibility when man willingly joins in as a junior partner in God's affairs. Man's responsibility in the partnership is to help make the change effective. The question is, will he?

God's kind of change is not reserved for the distant by and by. It is now. Instead of allowing our todays to lie in bondage to the regrets of yesterday and the fears of tomorrow, Jesus proclaims, "The kingdom is at hand." God's future is the magnet that draws man's present into being. Thus Jesus sees God's love as the presence that allows human personhood to emerge and grow. Referring to the earthly father who knows how to give good gifts to his children, Jesus asks his disciples, ". . . how much more will the heavenly Father give the Holy Spirit to those who ask him!" (Luke 11:13). And to Zacchaeus he announces: "Today salvation has come to this house" (Luke 19:9).

The central theme of Jesus' teaching is the kingdom of God. In his ministry and message Jesus makes it clear that he is concerned with nothing less than the renewal of the world along the lines of God's original architecture. The program Jesus undertook in his earthly ministry is concisely described in Mark 1:15 (Phillips): ". . . Jesus came into Galilee, proclaiming the gospel of God, saying, 'The time has come at last—the kingdom of God has arrived. You must change your hearts and minds and believe the good news.'" What a change this call brought to the lives of those who responded! Two fishermen left their nets to summon men for Christ. A tax collector left his lucrative position to follow Jesus. Perhaps the most remarkable personality among the disciples, Peter, experienced a change that led into a lifetime of change and growth.

As we face change, it is easy enough to fall captive to fear. If we lose what we have, what awful thing will take its place? But we can be set free from such fears when we know Christ as Lord over all. In this freedom we can dare to venture into new ways of taking on emerging problems. Change may not come easily to us as Christians, but it can come. As a rather homely example, when motion pictures first appeared, some religious leaders feared them as a "work of the devil," but today films have become an important tool in communicating the Christian gospel.

Fear of change played a large part in the efforts of Jesus' opponents to frustrate his mission. It is evident that leaders in the social structure of Jesus' day felt threatened by his declaration of "good news to the poor." How, except as a rude gesture of hostility, can we explain the action of the Pharisee who invited him to be a dinner guest and then omitted the usual courtesies accorded by the servants? Jesus was celebrity enough to be invited; threat enough to be put in his place socially.

Obviously Jesus upset the expectations of the "pillars of the church" by the way he fulfilled his calling as a religious teacher. They accused him of all sorts of things: "Look, a drunkard and a glutton—the bosom-friend of the tax-collector and the sinner" (Matthew 11:19, Phillips). His conflict with the Judaism of his time was much more than a splitting of hairs over interpretation or program. Such a dispute would hardly have led to his death. Rather, the issue was the presence of a new authority, as evidenced in the total work of Jesus. Jesus' ethic of love had threatened the traditional authority of the Jewish law.

Many of the parables of Jesus are about God's future which breaks into man's today. This day, Jesus says, is alive with God's tomorrow. It is like the unexpected fulfillment of a lifelong search. No wonder that the only way the apostle Paul could express it was with the description of "a new creation." If God's future is available right here and right now, why do we humans continue to live as so many beggars? We are made emotional paupers by our anxiety over problems like these: "Will we have enough to retire on?" "Are our savings big enough for a rainy day?" "We can't go in that old car (dress, hairdo, etc.)." Such questions express the "bigger and better barns" philosophy of life, and Jesus was pretty rough on it (Luke 12:13-21).

WHAT IS REQUIRED OF MAN?

What more did Jesus require of one who came across his future already available, than that he claim it? What of the man who plowed up the treasure chest on the back forty? What of the jeweler who found the pearl of exceptional quality? How did Jesus reply to the wealthy young man who came in search of eternal life? In each of these stories it was required only that the seeker should claim his treasure by accepting and doing God's will. The rich young man had already lived a life better than most men, but he was not ready to face the challenge of total commitment. He faced the choice we all face whenever God's possibilities intersect our own intentions (Luke 18:18-29).

All men are captives in the sense that they are limited to a particular time and place in human history, and the Christian is no exception. Nevertheless he can be an agent of change if he fits his limited lifetime into the eternal purposes of God, who is both the beginning and the end of all time and history.

What is required of us in order that we may know God? From Adam to Jesus there is a remarkable testimony that man comes to know God not primarily by thinking about him but by meeting him as a person. We come to know God when we come to trust him. It is when we refuse to trust him and to obey his commandments that we grow ignorant and begin to doubt his existence.

The study of God's Word can help lead us to such personal knowledge. A layman engaged in depth Bible study of Ephesians called his pastor early one morning and asked to see him immediately. They met before breakfast. "After studying the Bible, I've made a decision," the layman said. "I can't be honest with God or with myself if I don't do it." The pastor listened expectantly. The layman hesitated a moment. Then he blurted out his confession. "This morning just as soon as the office opens, I'm going to straighten things out with the Internal Revenue people. I've been cheating on my income taxes for four years, and now I'm going to clear matters up." Concerned study of the Bible had led this man to an important ethical decision. It had also opened new opportunities for a trusting relationship with the eternal God.

Rather than respond in total commitment, we often try to bargain with God. Perhaps the most popular form of such bartering is formal religious observance. We think we can work a deal with God. If the price of the good life is to go to church regularly and to behave decently, well, it seems fair, especially when you consider what we are getting in return. But we cannot get away with such dickering. If our relationship to God is limited to what we think is a good bargain, a nice deal, or a cozy arrangement, we miss out on the dynamic interrelationship with God that is so essential for creative living in times of tumult.

J. S. Whale sees the parable of the Prodigal Son as an illustration of how man tries to do business with God, "as though he were not the Holy Father but a banker keeping a debit and credit account." Both sons were guilty of such a commercial mentality—the younger son wanted to take out a bank loan while the elder brother preferred to open a savings account.⁵ When God offers all of the future to us, beginning today, we respond with nickel-and-dime morality and five-and-ten piety. Rather than allowing our todays to be captured by God's tomorrow, we try to cut his kingdom down to denominational thinness and into congregational cookie-cutter shapes.

A modern version of this denial of God's glory and sovereignty is the notion that today's science and technology have overcome nature and man at last has come into his own. Thus, some even write that man has finally "come of age." Not scientists, but their popularizers, are generally responsible for this easy optimism. Many of our best scientists stand in awe of the mysteries of the universe and repent of the inhumanities of man.

From this mood of confidence in man's own powers comes a tragic irony. On the one hand we assume that for collective man nothing is impossible. At the very same time, however, as individuals we feel trapped without access to the sources of power. While some men declaim with sincere confidence that finally man has achieved a mature civilization, countless millions of individuals wonder how to escape the traps of the same civilization.

This conflict between collective power and individual frustration was visible in a Washington seminar of college students during one phase of the Vietnam crisis. Fairly quivering with the electric sense of power, they interviewed key persons in government—Congressmen, Senators' assistants, and influential members of the Executive Branch. When, however, the conversation turned to specific national needs then prevailing (e.g., peace in Vietnam, or community services for urban ghettoes), these leaders of government expressed frustration that they lacked the power to act. The students went away feeling that while they had visited a great generator station, perhaps the largest power center in the world, the power plant workers had never seen the little room that turned the power on and off. Even in the White House, if we are to judge from what we read, a sense of frustration is often present. So much power, but the individual often feels unable to manage it!

And yet, how dependent human beings are upon one another! One of the most powerful individuals in the world, though he inhabits the White House, is directly linked with the peasant mother in a Vietnamese hovel. Politics didn't make it that way. God intended that it should be that way. People find themselves by the very nature of life to be related to each other in significant and specific situations. The traditions and customs which a particular society or culture develops as formal patterns for governing these relationships are called "structures." These are accepted as the ways things are done. Structures define such things as the relationships between the sexes, the responsibilities of providing for family needs, and the bases of social position and personal power. Such structures influence how we look at life and what we purpose to do with what we are and what we have.

How should man relate to the structures of his particular culture? Should he accept them, or should he try to change them? Christians find in Jesus Christ a person who was able to draw the line when the traditions and institutions of his day conflicted with his larger loyalty to God. The faith of the Christian in any age must lead that individual to follow the will of God as he personally understands it, whatever the existing structures.

As we continue our inquiry as to whether man is the victim or the author of social and technological change, let us consider the relation of God as Creator to his creation and his creatures. In faith we affirm that we can discern God's will and activity in many of the events in human history, for God is using history to bring into reality his concerns. Therefore we look for the places where God is lifting up and tearing down, redeeming and preserving, judging and rebuilding. We recognize that we must come to grips with contemporary issues in the light of God's revelation.

We have seen how Jesus in his human life demonstrated the possibility of living obediently in God's creation and relationally with one's fellowman. This same Jesus also had to live in relation to structures such as the Roman Empire, particularly the regional government headed by Pontius Pilate, and the religious and social systems of his time, such as those of the Pharisees and Sadducees and of Jewish people in general. Nevertheless his allegiance was to something greater than political loyalty or national sovereignty. His daily dependence was upon God.

Human life is a combination of independence and interdependence. Man finds himself incomplete unless he is in relation with others. Even those who have deliberately isolated themselves from their fellows cannot logically overlook their dependence upon the world for their basic physical needs. Even the ancient recluse Simeon Stylites, who spent thirty years of his life atop a sixty-foot pillar, still needed someone to bring him food and water.

One of the unsuspected blessings of urbanization is that we are constantly reminded of our interdependence. Perhaps one responsibility of the church in our modern society is to point up this interdependence by demonstrating what it means to be responsibly related to one another. This humanizing function of the Christian community within our urban culture is a necessary and important contribution.

MAN OR BEAST?

Man's response to creation and to his fellowman involves questions like these:

What do I make of the universe? Does all of this hold any significance or meaning? Surrounded by the world and all these other people, who am I? Does my life have meaning?

Such questions seem to remain constant concerns for man's introspective moment. William Golding has dealt with them in his novel *Lord of the Flies,* the story of a planeload of British schoolboys whose plane crashes on a tropical island. All adults aboard the plane have perished. As the only humans on the island, the boys improvise what social organization there is. At first they make rational decisions after something like democratic discussions, but the little veneer of polite society is soon worn away and the boys form into tribes. As petty differences, magnified through fear and suspicion, become major antagonisms, the boys degenerate into warring savages and finally to demon-haunted murderers acting on irrational impulse. A bloodbath is averted only through renewed contact with the adult world in the form of an arriving British warship. Thus order is restored in the boys' realm, but in the image of the warship the reader is left with the awareness of a hate-filled chaos beneath the surface of humanity.

Many such novels and plays today argue that such animalism is the sum of human existence. Scratch the average man or boy, they say, and you discover a hedonistic savage who is ready to do anything to his brother in order to satisfy himself. He is seen as Cain still rising up against his brother to kill him.

Has man made any ethical progress since the days of Cain? A more encouraging answer is offered in Ernest Gordon's *Through the Valley of the Kwai,* which like *Lord of the Flies* deals with the cultivated Britisher away from his carefully maintained civilization. There the similarities end. Golding deals with boys, Gordon with men. Golding writes fiction, whereas Gordon relates real life.

Ernest Gordon was one of the war prisoners in World War II assigned by the Japanese to work on the infamous railroad bridge over the River Kwai. The place where he was interned was more of a death camp than a prisoner-of-war camp, and under these brutal circumstances the men for a time acted little better than the boys of Golding's book. When new prisoners were brought in, the old prisoners mobbed them and stripped them of boots, shirts, trousers, utensils —anything of value. When a prisoner became too ill or dejected to fight for his few belongings or meager daily ration, the stronger men would take these from him, thus hastening death. In this terrible prison camp man seemed on the way to becoming a marauding animal of the lowest form.

Then something happened to change the life pattern of the entire prison camp. There was a Scot soldier, an Argyll, who according to the custom of his people had a "mucker," a pal with whom he shared everything he had. Angus' mucker lay near death, and the human vultures were descending on him. But Angus remained loyal. When his mucker's blanket was stolen, he gave him his own. After a hard day's work, Angus would come and tend his mucker's wounds and give him his own food ration. At night Angus would risk his life to slip by the prison guards and into the jungle villages nearby in order to barter for vegetables and eggs with which to nourish his mucker. Angus was a big man, but the combination of hard work, little food, and no rest took their toll on him at last. Just as his mucker began to regain his health, Angus fell over and died. The camp doctors diagnosed the cause of death as "starvation complicated by exhaustion." As the soldier who told Gordon the story said, "He mucked in with everything he had—even his life."[7] This example of self-sacrifice turned the whole camp away from its rush toward chaos, and gradually a better community was built.

These two books dramatically contrast the Christian view of life with its opposite. Both Golding and Gordon see the real nature of the human predicament as sin and evil. Man will misuse his freedom to deny or take away his neighbor's freedom. Man is capable of exploiting his fellows in beast-like fashion. Yet Golding finds no rescue from this churning evil except the arrival of a warship, whereas Gordon sees in the history of the prisoners a working out of salvation through the power of self-giving love.

The discovery by these war prisoners of the person of Christ through study of the New Testament demonstrates vividly the way in which the gospel intersects men's lives at their points of persistent need. We see in these men of the Kwai a growing awareness of dignity, meaning, and value possible not only despite suffering but through bearing the sufferings of others. It is a highly realistic interpretation, for sacrificial love is essential if real reconciliation is to take place among persons in society.

An Austrian psychotherapist who survived a terrifying experience in the Nazi concentration camps wrote:

> Man *can* preserve a vestige of spiritual freedom, of independence of mind, even in such terrible conditions of psychic and physical stress. We who lived in concentration camps can remember the men who walked through the huts comforting others, giving away their last ｊiece of bread. They may have been few in number, but they offer sufficient proof that everything can be taken from a man but one thing: the last of the human freedoms—to choose one's attitude in any given set of circumstances, to choose one's own way.[8]

MAN CAN CHOOSE

This conscious choice of how one responds to any given situation is essential to a Christian understanding of human nature. Whether in the extreme condition of the concentration camp or the more common situation of stress within daily routines, man is faced with decisions. To drift, allowing the situation to resolve itself, or to let others decide in the void of one's own nondecision, is not the stance of the Christian faith but the slouch of lethargy.

The Christian understands that maturity involves responsible decision—conversion, if you will. He is called to take the initial steps toward a total process of radical change. Conversion, as de Rougemont suggests, is an "individual revolution,"[9] Yet it is more than this. Conversion is a response to the power that enables a person to move beyond concern with himself alone to a lively, life-giving concern for others. Hans-Reudi Weber was one of the first to speak of the need for a "double conversion," first from the world to Christ, and then with Christ into the world; and the dean of evangelists, Billy Graham, has cited this observation in addressing the National Council of Churches. Christian decision is not "once and for all" but rather "once, and then for all others." When we give ourselves in faith as disciples of Jesus Christ, we find that just as he gave himself for others, so we are now increasingly enabled to give of ourselves for the sake of others.

As Jesus told Nicodemus so many years ago, a new birth is essential if man's real being is to emerge into life. The new person who comes into being through Christ is oriented toward a future rich with God's possibilities. The born-again believer lives with a positive and purposive expectation of God's coming into man's personal life as well as his social relationships. The believing Christian does not know *what* is coming in the future, but in faith he does know *Who* is coming. This new person in Christ is a new kind of man, already sharing in the future which God makes possible through his redeeming love—the love that sets men free.

5 *THE CROSSING POINT*

TO GROW UP the young person needs to step forward on his own, to try to live his life without always asking his parents or age-mates, "What shall I do?" As he continues to mature, he must also move beyond preoccupation with his own needs, desires, and self, lest his ego become his prison. In becoming sensitive to others, the mature person does not surrender his own individuality. Rather, through increasing service to others he finds a larger arena for the expression of his own maturing self.

Whether the self develops in relation to others or stagnates in self-encircled concern, the reality of evil and suffering hammers on the consciousness. One consequence of creation is that man is a part of the world as it exists. He shares the responsibility of all men for the world and thus becomes free in it. Every man has the opportunity to live a life of decision, and he is free to make whatever decision he will, for good or evil. Therein lies the root of the human dilemma. Samuel Miller in his oratorio *What Is Man?* has described this freedom as the mark of Adam:

> My mark—God made it—
> My mark is freedom.
> God made it, never to be taken, else I be not man.

59

> Its burden is endless, sometimes bitter, but it is mine forever.
> Turn me not back from the sky
> But light me a star in this dark self.

How does one deal with this anguished cry? Has God, in conferring freedom on man, in granting virtual co-creatorship, weighed man down with an intolerable burden? It need not be so. The faith and the experience of Christians convincingly demonstrate that God does provide dynamic strength for decisive living.

The anguished concern, "Am I free or am I a puppet?" represents one of the issues that persist through all the years of a person's life. Wherever man raises such a cry, there is a possibility of a *crossing point*, a point of encounter between man and God. The crossing point may occur anywhere in life, but it is especially likely to be formed in the midst of change.

This term "crossing point" identifies a key concept in the newest curriculum resources for Christian teaching. One plane of the intersection is represented by the needs that man continually experiences through the whole of life. Examples include such issues as these: "What is freedom and how do I use it?" "Who am I?" "Am I a maker of decisions or am I a rubber-stamp?" "What does it mean to possess sexuality?" "What are the meanings and experiences of life that provide satisfaction and value for me?"

The second plane of the intersection is the gospel, which cuts across our lives and reveals reality in questions such as these: "What is the good news about man?" "How does God disclose himself?" "How has he made his power available to energize us for more creative living?" "What transforming power is present in the life, death, and resurrection of Jesus Christ?"

The crossing point occurs wherever the concerns of the Christian faith intersect the life of the learner at a specific point in his stage of development. The context for learning in the Christian faith is the dynamic interaction of the gospel with the concerns of the learner in all of his relationships. Within this context, then, the crossing point is reached *at the moment when we make our decisions,* and this is the very point or place *where we meet God.* Thus the place of decision making is the crossing point where God and man meet in the midst of change.

DECISION AS A CROSSING POINT

A quick look at that grand old man of faith in the Old Testament, Moses, may illustrate this concept. At what point did Moses become conscious that his concern had crossed paths with God's purpose? One such moment came during what must have begun as just another day for him. It was a moment of decision which he could only regard as an encounter with God. Certainly it did not come because Moses possessed an unusual capacity for piety. He was not performing his religious duties when he came to the "mountain of God" (Exodus 3:1) where he reached the crossing point. He came there on an ordinary work-day, just going about doing whatever it is that a shepherd does. Actually he stumbled upon the place without suspecting it to be in any sense holy.

How do we know there was a crossing point on that mountain that day? What really happened? What turned Moses into a person of destiny? Was there a meeting of an actual responsibility in history and the personal recognition of God as the initiator? The lesson of history is that in truth there *was* a crossing point of responsibility and response, for it turned Moses right around and sent him back into the political affairs of Egypt. What did Moses have to say to his fellow Hebrews? Did he possess some special knowledge regarding the divine mystery? Was there some new religious notion? No, it is simply that Moses plainly received his assignment: Go and read the signs of the times.

It was God who was moving toward the humans lying captive in Egypt. "I have seen the affliction . . . have heard their cry . . . I know their sufferings, and I have come down to deliver them . . ." (Exodus 3:7-8). Moses, challenged to respond, became an accessory to God's action in releasing the people of Israel from Pharaoh's jailhouse. In going because God had sent him, Moses acted in the capacity of a man of faith. In the words of Bernhard Anderson, ". . . the divine call to decision and responsibility is one of the characteristic notes of Israel's faith." [1]

Moses remains for us the classic example of man at the crossing point, one who meets God in the midst of change. In him we see what happens when *meanings meet*—the meanings for himself of his life experiences and the meanings for humanity of God's purposes. When God's purpose met with Moses' experience, history was redirected. Because Moses was finally persuaded to see what God meant, the captive people were set free from Egypt.

What we have seen in the experience of Moses illustrates the idea of the crossing point as the interaction of the Christian gospel with the persistent lifelong concerns of the learner. When this term appears in curriculum materials, it has a similar meaning. Sometimes, in error, we have tried to make two separate packages of the gospel and life, packages which look very much alike but actually remain separate and different.

Just the opposite is intended by the idea of the crossing point. Life is not the only source of experience, nor is the gospel the only source of meaning. There is also experience in the gospel and meaning in life. The crossing point has to do with the *meeting of meanings:* The meaning of the gospel is experienced as our life's experience acquires meaning.

NOT THIS: BUT THIS:

Man's life is filled with crossing points. God continued to speak to Moses many times after that first dramatic incident on the mountain. The apostle Peter, long after the day on which he was called from his fishing, continued to discover new challenges in the teaching of Jesus and in the leading of the Holy Spirit. For each of these men, as for us, the same issues persist through life, though they may show up in different ways. So the gospel continues time and again to intersect our life's concerns at critical points. The intersections are apt to occur at irregular intervals and with varying force and relevance, but in each of them the eyes of faith can discern God's concerns cutting across the issues of man's life.

From the diagram which follows we can get a rough idea of the way in which crossing points occur. The solid line represents the gospel, that is, the content of the Christian faith; and the broken line signifies man's life span, with its persistent issues. Although at all times the lines are close, there are certain points at which their meanings are closer than at others, and several (such as those marked by X) where they actually intersect.

The diagram suffers from limitations. Life is more of a process and the gospel is far more dynamic than a series of neat loops suggests. The diagram achieves its purpose, however, if it helps us to recognize that crossing points occur again and again through life. Just so long as man has needs (in other words, all through life), and just as long as God cares about man (that is, through all eternity), man's needs and God's love will find intersection. Hallelujah!

Think again about the crossing point which Moses experienced on the mountain. All of Moses' life—past, present, and future—acquired new meaning when God's word crossed his burning issues. It was a meeting of Creator and creature in which change occurred and new learnings were achieved. Wherever such a meeting really occurs, there is the potential for similar results.

This idea of the crossing point has important consequences for Christian education. A learner will become deeply involved in any community of learning only when he perceives the meaning and value of the gospel for him *right now* in his own life situation. Recognizing this principle, the sensitive teacher plans, teaches, and evaluates his work, asking such questions as: "What does this information or activity mean to the learner?" "Why is it of value to him?" "How does it help him to live?" "Why is it significant?" The purpose of creating teaching-learning opportunities is to communicate experience and meaning at the crossing point, where dynamic interaction between the gospel and the concerns of the learner is taking place. "Gospel" here suggests God's whole continuous redemptive action toward man, known especially in Jesus the Christ. "Concerns" refers to the persisting issues of a person's life experience in his whole field of relationships. These include his relation to God, to his fellowman, to the natural world, and to history.

Christian education is concerned with more than having the growing person "take notice." He is not just to "sit and get," but to "do and act" in his fullest capacity as a son of the Creator.

Here is an example of the crossing point in modern life. The scene is a remote section of Harlem, forgotten even by New Yorkers, a catch-basin for the dropouts from life, a place where not a single household on the block would fit the usual description of "family." The area was so bad that the city fathers had decided that the only solution for its problems was to tear the neighborhood down. In the face of this decision, however, something happened in that little ghetto within a ghetto. Partly because of the ministry of Chambers Memorial Baptist Church and partly because the people who lived there recognized that they were the social rejects of the big city—for these, and what other reasons no man knows—the people began to stir! Apathy slowly, painfully was replaced by political concern. It was ineffective, disorganized, fragmented, but the people were doing something, these tag-ends of humanity who had never accomplished much in the past. As a last resort to save their street from the wrecker's crane, the community organized a delegation to visit City Council in session. When the Vice-mayor made a statement criticizing the neighborhood, a woman from Chambers Memorial asked for her right as a citizen to challenge the error in his remarks, and she was recognized. As the group later left the Council chamber, the woman was jubilant. She had dared to speak up to this power-figure in defense of her neighbors.

Because of this event a woman had discovered that she was a person! She had value. She possessed dignity. She recognized that she too could be a leader, a spokesman for the feelings of others. Only those who have worked with the apathetic, the outcasts living without hope, can sense the miracle in this woman's discovery of her personhood. The main persistent life issue for her was "Who am I as a person?" A crossing point occurred at the Council meeting, for it was then that she grasped and acted upon the meaning for her of the gospel theme, "Christ came as a servant and calls us to servanthood." Nurtured within the Christian fellowship, she was prepared for a meeting of meanings when it took place in a public situation.

Another example of the crossing point is seen in the experience of a man who for years had been an avid reader of pornographic literature. "The dirtier the books, the better," he admitted. His fellow workmen on the power-line crew always knew he could provide them with a smutty novel. Though a churchman for many years, he had sensed no conflict of values. One day, however, the witness of the Christian community against this type of reading broke through to him. Here was a crossing point. The nurture of the church school and the meaning of worship which had built up in his life over a period of years, now helped him to see reality. He recognized that his addiction to reading about cheap sex was a form of bondage. In an act of religious commitment he threw off the fetters that had so long bound him to pornography.

What happened as a result of this change? He was a radically new personality. His wife said so, and his children showed their response in their own lives. He began to enjoy, as never before, the whole of life, including the intimate relationship God intended husband and wife to enjoy. What of his fellow workmen? Even though their source of dirty books was suddenly dried up, they too expressed their satisfaction that he was a new person. They actually liked him better now that he was free.

Let's take this true experience and follow down the lines that lead to the intersection. What was his persistent need, the issue in his case? It was to be a person who stands in freedom and dignity. He had felt this need since childhood and would continue to face it in new ways as he continued in his mature years. What word did the gospel offer? The love and power of God, always available in Jesus Christ, is able to set us free from servitude. For this man, reading about cheap sex was a prison. When he realized his imprisonment, he also recognized that Christ could release him from such bondage. He then became a man able to express his personality as well as his sexuality as husband, father, fellow workman, and Christian.

Crossing points may come at all ages. A first-grader, after making a classmate cry by laughing rudely along with the rest of the class at the other child's poor reading ability, has a meeting of meanings in which he walks over to the classmate and places his arm comfortingly around him. A teen-age girl admits frankly to her church youth group that she has been smoking for the specific purpose of attracting attention of a questionable nature, and now she decides that such a strategy is incompatible with her faith. Another teen-ager, deeply moved in her resistance to her nation's military operations overseas, willingly incurs the wrath of the school authorities by refusing to salute the flag at school. Persistent life concerns, in these situations as well as in the adult crossing points we have already cited, are encountered in varying forms at various ages, but the basic issues go on through the years awaiting encounter with the gospel at times of crisis.

A congregation can help persons to prepare for living in the midst of change as its educational ministry allows them to develop their God-given capacities for leadership. Especially, it can help them to grow in their ability to make decisions. Though such growth occurs in various ways, actual participation in decision making is ultimately the only really effective way in which persons become decision makers. The Christian faith gives us such experience as it requires us to work at harnessing the dynamics of change to the purposes of God.

RESOURCES OF THE GOSPEL

Three elements of the gospel which often relate directly to the crossing point are grace, hope, and confidence in God. As these intersect the situations of life, they may create patterns of successive crossing points. Let us think about each of these resources and what they can mean in human life.

Grace is God's love actively directed toward man for the sake of man's well-being. As the Christian lives from day to day in a state of continuing dependence on God, God's grace strengthens him and enables him to live creatively. Paul wrote, ". . . let us continue at peace with God through our Lord Jesus Christ, through whom we have been allowed to enter the sphere of God's grace, where we now stand" (Romans 5:1 N.E.B.). Grace here means God's intention that our lives shall be creative, productive, and joyous. Grace is his liberating love, always active to set us free from the limitations we face in the world. It is his constant effort to enable a life-receiving relationship between ourselves and him.

The grace which enables one to "sit loose" in the midst of life's urgencies can be expressed in nonreligious terms: John Gardner writes, "A meaningful relationship between the self and values that lie beyond the self . . . is an essential ingredient of the inner strength that must characterize the free man. The man who has established emotional, moral and spiritual ties beyond the self gains the strength to endure the rigors of freedom." [2] It is refreshing to hear this secular recognition of the grace-endowed relationship to God which the Christian would describe in more theological terms.

Hope is a second resource of the gospel for man at the crossing point. The freedom of man, in harness with the grace of God, provides for the open-endedness of history which always offers opportunity and gives man hope. The Christian sees Christ as providing this opening into the future. We are a people with a future, precisely because the future is God's and we are God's people. Viktor Frankl testifies out of his death-camp experience that "It is a peculiarity of man that he can only live by looking to the future," [3] and John Gardner similarly writes: "No society is likely to renew itself unless its dominant orientation is to the future." [4]

The Christian faith is directed toward the future. The prayer Jesus taught his disciples, "Thy kingdom come, Thy will be done, on earth as it is in heaven," and the parables of the Lord returning to his household at any moment accentuate the future note which is at the very center of the gospel. The prophets of the Old Testament gave the New Testament church this sense that the unity of history depends wholly on God. The Bible declares that history does possess a goal, and this is to be found in a kingdom of God to be established on earth. The prophets understood, and the early church experienced, that history in the making is always dynamic and points beyond itself. It is filled with hope. In Christ, God has fully entered into the history of man and promises his continuing action in all future history as long as time endures. God himself is to reign beyond the ends of time and space as the eternal reality providing meaning for man's pilgrimage.

This Christian attitude of historically founded hope for the future has practical consequences. Hope provides man with adequate goals. When we recognize that we as individuals are highly valued by God, we grasp that death is not the conclusion of all things for us. Our lives are no longer regarded as beginning in chaos and ending in nothingness, but rather as purposefully granted and guided by God. Thus the Christian hope illuminates the profound meaning of Jesus' deceptively simple words: "The market price of five sparrows is two cents, isn't it? Yet not one of them is forgotten in God's sight. . . . Don't be afraid, then; you are worth more than a great many sparrows!" (Luke 12:6-7, Phillips).

Christian hope also provides a critical clue to the problem of suffering. As the Christian contemplates the cross of God's most dearly beloved, he senses a possibility of meaning in human suffering which often baffles the nonbeliever.

Confidence in God, the third resource, is the partner of hope. When we can look hopefully into the future, we can also feel confident in him who guides our planning and working. Optimism about the future allows realism in the present and stimulates good use of the time and resources now available. A sensitive schoolteacher noted this factor in children with whom he worked:

> Intelligent children act as if they thought the universe made some sense. They check their answers and their thoughts against common sense, while

other children, not expecting answers to make sense, not knowing what is sense, see no point in checking, no way of checking. Yet the difference may go deeper than this. It seems as if what we call intelligent children feel that the universe can be trusted even when it does not seem to make any sense, that even when you don't understand it you can be fairly sure that it is not going to play dirty tricks on you. How close this is in spirit to the remark of Einstein's, "I cannot believe that God plays dice with the universe." [8]

Precisely this confidence in God makes possible creative interaction with others, with nature, and with the world of ideas. This is an important insight into how man can use change rather than be abused by it. Certainly the Christian, secure in knowing that God is Lord over changing history, can move confidently within the rapid flow of human events. It is this confidence that gives a Christian the long view that permits him to have mature anticipations.

6　LOVE IN LEARNING

IN ITS TEACHING MINISTRY TODAY the Christian church is called to help persons become flexible enough to respond effectively to change. A substantial investment of love on the part of those who teach will be needed if this type of learning is to take place, but this investment is essential if the church is to minister in a world where responsive and responsible personalities are needed as leaders and change shapers.

In order to discuss the place of love in the learning experience, it may be helpful to define what is meant by the key words "learning" and "love."

WHAT IS LEARNING?

Learning is the generating, changing and redirecting of attitudes, understandings, and action patterns through experience. A couple watched their baby daughter learn to eat with a spoon after they had despaired for months that she would ever acquire this skill. The great event occurred when some friends, a young family with a daughter of the same age, stopped overnight while traveling through the city. At dinnertime the little visitor spoon-fed herself with great skill and drew many compliments for this ability. The other child was all eyes and ears, and before the evening meal was over, she too had rejected all parental assistance and was managing her own spoon, thank you. The model of a child like herself provided motivation and enabled an experience in which she developed her own skill.

Learning is a process of human change, which results from what the learner experiences in all of his relationships. As he relates to God, his fellowman, the natural world, the events of history, and his own developing self-understanding, in all these relationships the learner engages in an ongoing process we call *becoming*. He is becoming the person that God potentially created him to be. In so doing he may change in his understandings, attitudes, and actions.

Some changes come because the body naturally grows, develops, and deteriorates; others because of the person's experiences. Learning is related mostly to those changes which come through experience. The basic learning task of Christian education, therefore, is twofold: to listen with growing alertness to the gospel and to respond in faith and love. Here the transforming power of God's Holy Spirit may be felt as the listener hears, accepts, and fulfills the demands of the gospel. Caught up in the dynamic of the gospel, he experiences the good news and knows the liberty it makes possible.

Learning can be a straight line of action and understanding which moves forward as the learner actively listens to the real world and the real gospel. This can produce further movement as a spiraling cycle of three additional learning tasks: exploring, discovering, and appropriating. These may come in any order, but often listening is followed first by exploration, as the person tries to find out more about himself and the world in which he lives. Next he may discover meaning and value in the self and in the world he is exploring. Finally, he may be ready to appropriate (make his own) what he has discovered, by assuming personal and social responsibility for its application. The cycle continues as the learner moves forward again in listening and so opens anew the possibilities of exploration and discovery. It might be diagrammed something like this:

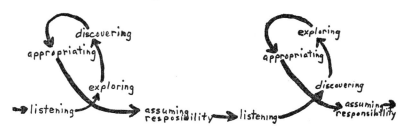

There is much discussion today as to what learning really is and how it takes place. Here are several ideas that are being advanced:

1. The learner must be ready to learn. Much has been made of such terms in public education as "reading readiness," which indicates that there is a certain point in a child's life at which his physical and mental development have brought him to the point where a new skill or understanding can be acquired. This principle is evident through life. There are many areas of learning which a person simply does not find challenging until he reaches a certain stage of maturity (for instance, sex interest, the nurture of children, and concern about death). The wise teacher takes such readiness into account.

2. Motivation is important, though not the kind which is provided by silver stars, candy kisses, attendance banners, or other devices which provide only a temporary satisfaction. The kind of motivation that leads to learning is the recognition that the personal interests or needs of the learner will be met in some significant way by the material to be learned. Continued learning takes place because the person has experienced satisfaction with his accomplishments and therefore is ready for more. As Jerome Bruner has remarked, the proper reward of learning is that we can use what we have learned.

3. There are both conscious and unconscious learnings. Some learning just "rubs off" on the learner. In any classroom or church a person may learn much that was not planned, along with the things he was intended to learn. In fact no teacher or preacher is always certain what is being learned, and even the learner may acquire something of which he himself is not aware. We are all familiar with the testimony, "He was hired by the school board to teach history, but he taught me how to be a man." Such unconscious teaching and learning can be good or bad; it can release us to live constructively or it may inhibit us with fears.

4. There are some learnings that reach the bull's-eye for which the teacher is aiming in the center of the learner's personal target and others that are off the edge. Thus we can speak of central (on-target) and peripheral (off-target) learnings. One child when given an assignment in a social studies workbook noted that the teacher regularly glanced through each page without reading it. So the child carefully filled in each line with a nursery rhyme. What had the child learned in using his workbook? Only the peripheral knowledge that he could fool a lazy teacher by filling up the page. He had missed the valuable insights which that work page contained.

When the learner recognizes that what he is learning is closely related to his persistent life concerns, he will regard it as useful and valuable. To acquire this learning he will expend his energies freely, perhaps even to the point of pain and struggle. The more radical a learning or change, the greater a learner's investment of self and energies will have to be—and, at the same time, the greater the change that can occur in the learner and the greater the possibility of permanent learning.

5. Learning may be either positive or negative or both. New attitudes, values, habits, or feelings may be helpful or harmful to further learning. In fact, sometimes there may occur changes in thought, feeling, or behavior which bottle up the further development and close down the potential for achievement. A series of positive learnings allows for an upward spiral, thus providing for development and growth, whereas negative learnings can cause regression or deterioration. One problem is that the teacher and learner will not always agree as to which learnings are positive and which are negative.

POSITIVE LEARNINGS PROVIDE DEVELOPMENT

NEGATIVE LEARNINGS HINDER MATURATION

What are some of the *ways* in which persons learn? They can be summarized as perception, problem solving, practice, and identification.

1. Perception has to do with both what one sees and the perspective from which he looks at it. Merely to pick up facts and skills is only the beginning of perception. The broader dimension involves his reflection and testing of this newly acquired material in terms of his relationships with things, people, and human events. For example, if through experience the learner has come to fear change, he will view every innovation with suspicion. On the other hand, if his past experience with change has been positive, he is likely to be more open-minded about the new idea or experience.

The fact that perception is more than merely seeing was demonstrated by a fifth-grade church school class who took a Sunday afternoon hike with their teacher, a professor of botany from the nearby university. Interested in the children and an expert in his field, he was able to point out features of the woodland that they had never before noticed. They had walked that path and seen those things in nature before, but this was the first time they had looked at them with understanding. Now for the first time, they perceived them. A noted philosopher has said, "It is one thing to have heard and read something, that is, merely to take notice; it is another thing to understand what we have heard and read, that is, to ponder."[1]

2. Problem solving involves the making of choices and decisions as the learner takes stock of a situation in light of his goals. He examines various ways of getting to a goal, considers the consequences of each, and decides which course he will take. He puts his decision into effect through action, taking full responsibility for the consequences. Finally he evaluates the consequences of what he has done by asking whether he has achieved the objective he intended.

3. Practice is the repetition of an activity to fix it in the learner's mind. Such repetition is of little value if it is merely mechanical; it must be recognized by the learner as purposeful. Therefore the teacher needs to inquire whether or not the practice is furthering the purpose of the learner. Is it helping him achieve his intended goal?

4. Identification means learning through relationship. Desiring to change in a certain direction, the learner may identify himself with some person or group that he admires, and thus will begin to make their values and goals his own. He may even adopt a person's entire style of life or model of ministry as his own. Learning by identification is not always intentional, however; it is often done unconsciously.

Any learning experience may involve change through any or all of these ways. Learning, while usually a gradual process, might occur quite suddenly. Some learning is so drastic that it has a powerful influence upon personality and often redirects the life orientation of the learner.

THE PLACE OF LOVE IN LEARNING

What is the role of love in learning? The superintendent of schools in a large midwestern city illustrated this in a conversation with the author by saying that most of the disciplinary problems brought to his attention arose out of a student's complaint that a certain teacher did not treat him fairly. "The teacher doesn't care about me!" the student would often complain. Were the feelings in these cases usually based on fact? The superintendent said that in the most serious disciplinary problems he had found, again and again the student correctly sensed the teacher's attitude. The student rebelled because he felt that he was being treated unfairly when the teacher did not care about him as a person—in other words, when he was not loved.

How would you define love? Erich Fromm has called it "the active concern for the life and growth of that which we love." [2] The New Testament pictures it as a relationship toward one's neighbor in which one sees, thinks of, and deals with his neighbor as Christ has acted toward each one of us. In both of these concepts we can see love as a caring for others, and thus it must be an important factor in learning. No doubt learning can occur in the absence of love, but the experience of successful teachers has demonstrated again and again that those who care about their students are the most effective.

Learning is helped by love and hindered by fear. A sensitive school teacher writes: "School feels like this to children: it is a place where *they* make you go and where *they* tell you to do things and where *they* try to make your life unpleasant if you don't do them or don't do them right." [3] He goes on to report from his observation that children do not see the primary business of the school day as learning, but rather as suffering through the routine chores that come up every single day. To do this with as little effort as possible and still avoid unpleasantness with the teacher is the name of the game. Later in his book the same writer drives home the point: "Even in the kindest and gentlest of schools, children are afraid, many of them a great deal of the time, some of them almost all the time. This is a hard fact of life to deal with. What can we do about it?" [4] Fear can and does frustrate the learning process.

On the other hand, love can release the person. Love can liberate from fear. When the teacher affirms the learner as a person, the dynamic powers within that person can be set free to assist him in his learning tasks. A public school teacher was teaching a second-grade reading group made up of slow readers. One boy had unusual difficulty. He began well enough, but after only two or three words he lost his initial speed. Every word, every letter required great effort. He seemed to find the consonants great hurdles to leap and the vowels long deserts to cross. It seemed that he would never complete the short sentence he was reading. Somewhere down in the depths of his little body a sound began. The teacher's stomach tightened as she felt the great effort he was putting into finding the sound that went with that word. Slowly, like a distant note from a subterranean river, the word began its hesitant progress. For a moment it appeared that the boy would abandon the desperate attempt. Then the teacher gently reached across and softly touched his cheek. And the word came!

The tender touch had affirmed the boy. It said to him, "You matter. You are worth much. I care that you express your worth." That teacher was doing more than just teaching a boy to read. She was helping to bring a person into being. "Perfect love drives out fear" (1 John 4:18, Moffatt).

Love makes a person open for learning. There is a liberating power in love. Lois Horton Young writes: "Loving a pupil means valuing him. . . . Every pupil is an important person; a wonderful person simply because he is valued for himself, not because he is attractive or 'smart' or well-behaved." [5]

Why is love crucial in Christian education? Our purpose, in any education that deserves to be called Christian, is to provide an experience in which the learner may encounter God. Our sincere expression of love frees this learner to accept God's searching after him and to respond to God in an individual human situation. It releases the personal powers of the learner. At the same time it also releases the teacher, allowing his full personhood to be open within the teaching-learning experience. Love further protects both teacher and learner from exploiting and using the other.

Not only does love permit this release of power, but, beyond this, the Christian faith sees love itself as a primary goal. Love is the reason, the meaning, the content of Christian learning. Mrs. Young, herself an effective teacher, says, "Excellent teaching methods and resources are greatly to be desired, but a teacher who cares about a pupil, genuinely values him and truly loves God with heart, mind, soul, and strength communicates to the learner what the best of materials and equipment cannot." [6]

The question is sometimes asked: Can the Christian way of life be taught? Obviously not, if teaching is to be done only through objective knowledge. There are no magic phrases, no lists of do's and don'ts, no equations or formulas which, once mastered, automatically make a person Christian. The Christian way of life cannot be memorized and "passed" in written examinations. Rather, it requires that a person be brought into being. When the pupil discovers that he is valued as a person, then (and only then) his potential for being starts on the road to full realization.

If children cannot be taught by conventional methods to have Christian personalities, then how does Christian education take place?

Mainly by experiences which occur in an atmosphere of love. Learning, in this sense, is the response of one person to another person. It is a *teaching-learning experience.*

The teaching-learning experience is as endless in its varied possibilities as are the many different situations in life. Children and teacher read a story together. The children may help to write a story, using their own skills and imaginations to build a new piece of literature. They may act out a story. They may learn through playing together, sharing their toys, or play-acting in a housekeeping corner. Young people or adults may learn about themselves and about life as a whole through drama and play reading, or through relationships with others in work projects. For people of all ages worship is an essential experience in learning as it allows for meditation, self-examination, and expression through reading, singing, and bodily movements.

We have mentioned that learning takes place through exploration and experience. The security that love makes possible enables the learner to be free to ask questions, especially the ones that are most important to him. Secure through knowing he is loved, the learner need not be defensive or fear that he might ask the "wrong" questions. He dares to ask anything at all regarding himself, his surroundings, or the universe, because love frees him to dare to explore all areas of life.

This release from fears and inhibitions is as necessary for the teacher as it is for the learner. If the teacher shares in a community of love and acceptance, he is freed of anxious concern as to whether the learner is asking the "right" question, and he can allow the teaching-learning situation to develop as it will. Rooted in love, the teacher is free to admit that he does not have all the answers. He can recognize his own doubts, his own share of wrong questions and wrong answers. He does not have to be defensive toward his students.

What does it mean to love? An excellent science teacher told a colleague, "You don't have to love your students to teach them." Many people would consider this statement to be a partial truth at best. If love is expressed, as Erich Fromm has suggested, by care, responsibility, respect, and knowledge, then perhaps even this "objective" teacher of purely scientific facts does love his students more genuinely than he is willing to acknowledge.[7] He is honest and responsible toward them in his use of facts, he respects their abilities to learn and grow, and he does try in some measure to know them. The Christian idea of education, however, goes beyond the "floor" of this minimal and rather academic kind of concern and rises to a ceiling limited only by the capacity of teacher and learner to share in God's love.

What are some of the ingredients of love? We may identify a few:

—*Partnership* suggests mutual sharing. Love clearly requires both giving and receiving. Jesus both accepted the ministrations of a woman washing his feet (Luke 7:38) and performed a similar service for his disciples (John 13:4).

—*Openness* gives love a quality of free exchange. We are honest and aboveboard in relationships that show love. We are not trying to sell anything or prove anything; we can be what we really are.

—*Trust* is involved in openness, for we place ourselves in trust to the other and we hope to receive his trust in return. We do not use our knowledge of the other to exploit his weakness or to manipulate his strength.

—*Acceptance* is another important element in love. We accept a person because of what he is as a child of God, and not because he is clever or cute or well-to-do. Acceptance is not the easiest quality to attain, but as we learn to accept others for what they are, we will discover an increase in love.

—*Freedom* develops in our relations with other persons and groups as a result of openness, trust, and acceptance. Love sets us free to be ourselves instead of being forced into a mold formed by our age-mates or our social group. It also makes us aware of the need for others to be free, and therefore we avoid trying to force *them* into *our* molds.

The essential requirement in love is to value the person loved. To value someone is to offer a basic affectional quality which is much more than sticky sentimentality. If one says to another, "I love you," or "I value you," then he should also be prepared to say, "I like you." Love that does not include valuing and liking is of little use in the church's educational ministry.

Love has a profound role in all of life's social relationships. As Christians we might well examine the questions put to love by the social upheavals of our day. If we are serious about love as value and affection, we must inject this powerful force into the great political, social, and economic problems of our times. Disorders in great cities and uprisings in small nations will not necessarily be solved with counter-force. Christians today are called to deal in love with the questions raised about the place of the oppressed and the meaning of their oppression. God's answer in Christ was a love which was willing to suffer for equality and justice—an awesome and costly love which led to a brutal cross. Are we ready to offer a love that seeks to express this spirit? [*]

Our concern for the learner needs to be more than just the question, "Is he getting the subject matter or not?" We need to care about how he feels about his learning or his failure to learn, and how he sees his relationship to his teacher, his fellow learners, and himself. We need to cultivate the ability to see the learner as he is and to be aware of his unique personality. The learner deserves our authentic respect, our just regard for his person and his abilities to develop. We need always to care enough to ask whether or not a teaching-learning experience is really taking place.

In terms of what we do in the classroom, Christian love will lead us to ask with real concern, "What makes *this* Stevie tick?" By trying to understand him more fully, by knowing his family, by being acquainted with his public school situation—this is the way we give of ourselves to Stevie in love. We are primarily interested in Stevie as a person and not in what we want him to get.

To emphasize the place of love in learning does not, of course, mean loss of content in the teaching-learning experience. Rather, the communication of content is enhanced by the sharing of an experience between the learner and the teacher. What is taught is not mere objective information for its own sake, but content of a kind which will enrich the life style of the learner. He will doubtless acquire many useful facts in the process of learning at this deeper level, but these are incidental to his main educational achievements in the area of attitudes—loving, respecting, caring, and responding—and their relationship to his own life concerns.

7 CHRISTIAN EDUCATION AS EXPERIENCE

IT HAS BEEN SAID we learn to swim in winter and to ice-skate in summer. During the off-season, when we are not actively practicing these muscular skills, our minds are at work consciously or even subconsciously considering the things we did a few months ago (like how we shifted our weight or how we cupped our hands). As a result of this delayed-reaction kind of learning, we are delighted to find that we have greatly increased our skill when the season returns.

Christian education resembles this process more than some of us have realized. The "season" for active study of the gospel and its meaning may occur only once a week, but the learnings of the larger world outside the church walls continue during the intervening days—in the public school, for instance, or in sports, business, or even in our experiences with the arts. The insights of Bible study, stored away in our memories, emerge and become personal as we reach crossing points where our secular experiences or learnings call upon them.

The learnings arising from Christian teachings become "whole" in a life-situation experience. The facts and ideas may be talked through in the church school class and the implications may even be "tried out" in a religious setting, but the certifying action is elsewhere. Life is whole, embracing both sacred and secular, and the teaching and learning of Christian faith and work must give recognition to this wholeness.

Meaning is most likely to be experienced sometime after the planned teaching-learning event and often at some distance from it. An adolescent, for instance, may have discussed "playing fair" and may have even looked up Micah's famous words, ". . . what does the Lord require . . . but to do justice, and to love kindness, and to walk humbly with your God?" (Micah 6:8), yet not until he reaches the locker room or the laboratory at school may his experience have a crossing point with the prophet's meaning.

Sensitive teachers make their lesson plans open-ended for each learner to apply the learnings in his own unique life situations. The learner himself is usually better able than the teacher to know how any new idea applies to his own life involvements. Those of us who are teachers in the church's ministry of education must sense the humility of our calling. Ours is to stimulate in the direction of shared goals. In this way we allow the meanings to surface in the life of the learner. Ours is to help the learner to become sensitive to the meanings of the gospel, not to prescribe where and in what fashion they will appear in his life.

PARTNERS WITH PUBLIC EDUCATION

Formal learning among children and youth takes place mainly in the secular setting of the public school. What the church teaches, therefore, even though it is most influential, must be seen as supplementing the growing person's day-to-day formal learnings. The learning experiences of the Sunday or weekday church school will be both tested directly in the secular classroom setting and filtered through the mental grid which has been established in the learner by the public school teaching. Public instruction may produce either a positive or negative setting for religious learning. Most likely there will be elements of both, but the important thing is not to evaluate its "goodness" or "badness" so much as to understand how the Monday-through-Friday educational experiences interact with those of the church.

If, for example, the student is fortunate enough to have public school teachers who encourage him to search openly for the truth in the whole of nature and history, he can be expected to bring this free and seeking attitude into the church school and youth activity. If, on the other hand, he is subjected in public school to a fact-oriented kind of teaching or a "pay attention to your elders and superiors" attitude, this stance toward learning will likely affect what he hears or does not hear in his study of the Christian faith.

Public education shapes the attitudes and expectations which the learner brings into the church context. Public education sets boundaries or possibilities for new learnings, and the Christian educator must either accept these boundaries or find ways to expand them. In some situations the public classroom limits the capacity of the pupils for personal development by teaching regional pride, uncritical nationalistic jingoism, and social patterns of conformity. In such cases we can usually detect the workings of prejudice on the part of a social class or an opinionated teacher. On the other hand, often it is the public school which is ahead of the churches in providing opportunities for growth and learning. In either case the church school leaders should examine their programs of study and activity to discover ways of allowing the gospel to be free to influence every area of the growing person's life.

The alert church school teacher will make an effort to discover what his students are studying, reading, and discussing in the public school. A perceptive public school teacher who has a class in the same age-group may be a helpful resource person. She may be the one person who knows most about what the child needs. She may be the person most aware of what parent and community problems exist. She may be the one who will be most helpful in determining how to handle the child's needs in personal encounter. An enterprising church school teacher will arrange an interview with this valuable resource person.

Another good source of help is the librarian, either at the school or at the public library. Librarians are most gracious, once they recognize that the church school teacher has come in the role of a learner and not that of a judge or censor of books. They can provide information as to what the children or young people are reading, and the teacher can gain many insights by browsing among these books.

Sometimes the church school teacher becomes discouraged because he has only an hour or two a week with his students, compared with the thirty hours or so which the public school teacher has available. Nevertheless, he should never underestimate the significance of this brief period of time. This is his opportunity to work in the area of the primary loyalties of persons, enabling his students to pull together all their experiences into a life system that will have lasting significance for them.

If the church school teacher sees his role as supplementing public education in the most intimate and personal area of life, that of commitment, an effective working partnership may develop with the public school teacher. This does not mean the church school teacher needs to know every public school teacher personally, but it does mean that he sees himself in partnership with public education. He seeks to be aware of what and how the professional educators are teaching as they encounter the church school students in their classrooms from day to day.

LEISURE AS A CLASSROOM

Leisure can also serve as a "classroom" for personal growth. The increasing amount of free time available today offers the individual a choice as to whether he will use this as an opportunity for growth or will yield to boredom and irresponsible activity "just for the sake of doing something." The word "leisure," however, has a tone which to many suggests especially the creative and developmental use of free time.

The child labor laws, which were a major development in social change during the early years of our century, introduced children and youth to free time. In general they seem to have made good use of it. They take music lessons, they go to ballet and drama rehearsals, they take part in choral groups. They are found in scouting and "Y" activities, athletic teams, and voluntary social services. They give many hours to the church. They are reading more, listening to music more, and traveling more. They are demonstrating that free time can be used for the creative development of their skills and personalities.

The increased free time which youth have enjoyed for a half-century or more is now also becoming available to adults with the coming of automation, cybernation, and affluence to modern life. The question is whether such free time is used for *leisure,* in the constructive sense in which we are using the word. Our society is fortunate in having many senior adults who are alert, growing, and useful persons. Leisure frees them to make a significant contribution to other people in a changing world where many willing hands and understanding hearts are needed in the area of service. One man who retired at the age of seventy-four spent the next decade using his former hobby as Mr. Fixit to bring a local church building into first-rate condition. His hours of effort allowed the church building to be used as a center of activity for a changing neighborhood.

Christian education, where it is vital, has made use of leisure as a means of encouraging personal growth. Nature has been a particularly effective resource. Some churches have organized day camps. Others have provided Saturday and Sunday nature hikes, during which minds and bodies are challenged to open up to the immense wonder of God's creation. Perhaps no development in America has had more profound social meaning than the tremendous expansion of church-sponsored summer activities. Ranging from formal conferences to informal camping, and including specialties like work camping, primitive camping, and rugged mountain trail camping, such experiences provide opportunities for growth in group living, intensive study, and increased appreciation of other faiths and cultures.

It is not surprising that many who commit their lives to church-related vocations or significant forms of nonchurch ministry in the world do so because of some summer experience. This is so for a number of important reasons. One of these is the tempo of the long slow days of summer. The hectic activity of our busy lives slows down, if for no other reason than the heat. A church conference or camp experience allows an opportunity for reflection on the long-term values of life. Furthermore, the very different "mix" of personalities attracted to a regional church camp or conference symbolizes silently the universality of God's love. Meeting new people, we are reminded that God has made many different kinds of persons, a whole world of them. Making new friends, we recognize the contagious character of friendship and see the vast possibilities of a lifetime devoted to building a more friendly world.

Service to others is an educationally significant use of one's leisure. The earliest Christians came to be known for their acts of ministering to persons in need. The parable of the good Samaritan illustrates the style of life inherent in the Christian faith. The idea of service to others, as the heart of the gospel, is caught not so much by telling as by actual participation in acts of service.

Christian education should include frequent opportunities for action. Talk is not enough. Action, rightly motivated, carefully thought out, and sensitively carried through, is a primary educational experience in the Christian faith. How will more adequate forms of neighborly assistance come about except through the actual practice of Christian goodwill toward persons with needs? When, for example, a pre-teen-age boy each week visits a ninety-year-old shut-in, both persons minister and are ministered to. The young Christian by engaging in ministry learns the meaning of Jesus' words, "you visited me." The elder Christian, in turn, experiences companionship and acceptance as he tells his young visitor tales of life in the past.

Young persons who are blessed by native intelligence plus superior educational facilities discover what it means to participate as well as share when they undertake to tutor students less favored than themselves. Such volunteer service not only gives the youthful tutors an experience of ministering, but it also arouses some profound questions in their minds: "What is meant when we say all men are equal?" "Why do I have such exceptional educational opportunities while others are neglected?" "What is my responsibility in the matter?"

Similarly, young persons who regularly undertake necessary tasks in hospitals, orphanages, and retirement homes discover that the act of ministering actually undergirds them with a larger experience. Quite often they discover that *they* have been ministered unto, even while carrying out their assigned ministries.

TEACHING THROUGH ART

There has been a cultural explosion in the modern world. Even the wasteland of television has occasional oases like Leonard Bernstein's Youth Concerts, educational TV's "What's New?" and childhood favorites like Captain Kangaroo and MisteRogers. And certainly the many new and illustrated books found in our expanding library systems are strong evidence of our growing interest in culture. Art is also a part of this expansion of cultural sensitivity. People in increasing numbers are painting pictures, modeling in clay, and visiting art exhibits. Art influences our mass magazines and even the design of our cereal boxes. Our children are perhaps better acquainted than we are with all forms of art—whether pop art, op art, the ashcan school, or the grand old masters.

Art is a medium by which the meanings of the gospel may meet with the persistent life concerns of the learner. The possibilities for crossing points can be increased as Christian educators reach out and explore new uses of art forms such as painting, sculpture, rhythmic movement, singing, and instrumental music. These can help both teacher and learner by allowing a means of tangible expression for a subtle concept. For instance, when a child expresses joy or hostility through the working of clay, he is able both to describe these feelings and to gain a healthy release. Art forms provide new ways of putting difficult and abstract ideas into a language understood by all ages, a language which is at once both physical and intellectual.

What place does art, in its many forms, have in Christian education? Here are six contributions art can make to the meeting of meanings, the crossing point of a person's concern and God's compassion.[1]

1. Art can increase our sensitivity to other persons. A nine-year-old boy, visiting an art museum with his father, came upon a modern impressionistic painting and remarked, "That picture looks like hell, Dad." Not knowing how to respond, the father simply uttered a noncommittal, "Oh," and changed the subject. Later that evening he asked the boy, "What did you mean about that picture, Dave?" "You mean the one about hell, Dad?" "That's the one. Why did you say that?" And then the boy recalled for his father an experience they had once shared in looking at some of the four-hundred-year-old woodcuts of the celebrated artist Albrecht Dürer. One such print described the torment of souls in hell. "What did you see in that modern painting that reminded you of Dürer?" the father asked. And the boy replied, "The faces were long and skinny and the look in their eyes was lonely, Dad, like the eyes in that old picture." The young child had correctly grasped the intent of the modern artist to portray the alienation of man from his fellows. It *was* hell, nothing less.

Through the centuries art has wrestled with the meaning of the reality that we bump into daily. When an artist conveys in his novel, play, music, sculpture, or painting his growing awareness of the human situation, he assists us to develop a sensitivity toward others.[2] Such films, for example, as *Cry, the Beloved Country,* which describes the torment that modern change brought to a Christian family in South Africa, allow the viewer a depth perspective on interpersonal and intercultural relations. Similarly, *The Pawnbroker,* which portrays the inability of a man to feel his neighbors' appeals for help because he has been so badly hurt in his own past, sensitizes us to the injury suffered by others.

2. The use of art in Christian education serves to broaden the imagination. Have you ever taken an eight-year-old child to a large city museum such as Chicago's Art Institute or New York's Metropolitan? One such child surprised his parents by insisting on returning again and again to stand before the grand staircase. The parents kept trying to drag him away. "Come look at this famous painting." Again, later: "Let's go look at the Egyptian mummies." Finally the parents decided to stop and see what it was that so absorbed the child. Then at last the adult mind was exposed to the grandeur of the architect's concept which the child had been admiring. The parents had seen the steps

only as something to be climbed, or better still to be avoided if they could find the elevator. But the child saw the grand stairway as the artist intended it, a work of art, drawing the spirit forward and upward, reaching to the heights of movement and aspiration.

Some artists have been critical of Elsie Anna Wood's portrayals of life in Bible times because they are "too literal," and yet these have transported many a Bible student into the reality of long-ago Bible lands. Even more forceful is the film *The Gospel According to Matthew,* which pictures Jesus in earthy sequences showing nonprofessional actors in dirty Mediterranean towns which are probably much more like the ones Jesus knew than the kind we see in antiseptic Cinemascope. Such interpretations help us to know a Jesus who lived among troubled people in a time of great political turmoil and whose ministry has meaning in similar conditions today.

3. The use of the arts provides an aid to reflection. All of us are accustomed to thinking about "how we are going to get this job done." Less frequently do we stop to ask reflectively, "What is the meaning behind this job, the meaning that underlies my doing it?" A group of adults at a laboratory school set an afternoon aside as a period for reflection. They spent the hours together in silence, working with their hands if they wanted to. Music was available from a collection of records. Books, paper, paste, crayons, paints, and modeling clay were all available on work tables. Many of the participants experimented in creative activity. A few wrote poetry. Some were surprised to discover that the use of their hands and minds in simple forms of painting and clay modeling allowed for mental reflection of a deeply satisfying quality.

4. The arts have the capacity to carry us beyond the limits of the tangible. Ours is possibly the first generation to spend its entire lifetime in a civilization dominated by technology. We think in technical terms and we set our goals in technical units. We even make our motor trips in terms of "driving hours" rather than persons to be visited or places of interest to be enjoyed. Technology asks fact-oriented questions like: "What is it for?" Art, however, traditionally has provided *meaning,* asking, "What's it all about?" Here art is in league with such theological questions as: "What is life?" "What is the eternal purpose in creation?" "What is man's role in the universe?"

5. Art forms help overcome barriers to understanding. The Dutch artist Rembrandt is universally appreciated, as is a Chinese Ming vase. Music provides an international language. Can you recall the first

Sunday on which you joined a congregation in singing the hymn "Joyful, Joyful We Adore Thee," set to a theme from the Ninth Symphony of the German composer Beethoven? Some have even found help in the songs of latter-day groups like the Beatles or the Mamas and the Papas, and a campus minister actually used the words of such iconoclastic songs of today as "Eleanor Rigby," "I Am a Rock," and "The Sounds of Silence" to bridge the generation gap.

6. Art allows us to extend ourselves beyond the present moment and place. Here it is locked in common purpose with the Christian faith, for both lift us out of this world and point to realms beyond, worlds yet to be explored. A group of Christians were exploring new forms in worship. Rhythm, the dance, the guitar (in place of the organ), folk songs, and songs of protest (along with traditional hymns) provided the content for the service of worship. The gospel lesson was read in the modern idiom from Carl F. Burke's *God Is for Real, Man.*[8] Here is the testimony of one member of the group:

> Worship provides for me a continuing central and crucial drawing together of each week. Yet I was appalled at how many protective barriers I have erected to keep from having the awesome holiness of God break through and demand something of me. My personal testimony is that some of these new forms of worship managed to penetrate the defensive maze of my soul.
>
> One particular: Near the close of the "new" service we were singing together the spiritual "Go Tell It on the Mountain." Just then three dancers came into the midst of the congregation with the great leaps familiar to ballet audiences. They moved in front of the communion table, down the long aisles of the sanctuary, and out into the world. Yes! my heart cried. Let's *do* tell it forth! Let's leap, let's go and sing, sing and shout the joyous good, good news!

Art has all of these possibilities for use within a creative effort in Christian education—and more!

8 THE CONGREGATION— RENDEZVOUS FOR MISSION

"THE BODY OF CHRIST takes up space on earth," wrote Dietrich Bonhoeffer.[1] We need to ask ourselves: What kind of space does our particular church occupy as an expression of Christ's body? Is it primarily a piece of real estate visible as a stone building next door to the savings bank and across the street from the supermarket? Or is it something else?

The biblical interpretation of the church is not as a building but as a people. In fact the apostle Peter calls the church "God's own people" (1 Peter 2:9). This image of a people possessed by God reflects a dynamic, pulsating, moving mass of humanity, a nation moving across God's earth on a definite pilgrimage with direction provided by the Creator himself.

If such a body takes up space, then the space is kinetic rather than static. It is space in action, going places and doing things. It is not just sitting in one place, bound by time or limited by geography. Christ's body takes part in God's action in history whenever and wherever the need arises. God's people are on the march. They have an important share in the action.

Why does God have a particular people called the church who take up space on the earth? The reason is clearly stated in passages such as Exodus 9:16 and Romans 9:17. These people are to declare God's love throughout all the earth. They are to be a visible, audible witness for all to see and hear. It might even be said that God's people are to be his advertisements on earth—his coaxing, singing, winning, persuading advertisements. They are to spread the word that God cares, and that he cares awesomely, about man.

Each of us can ask searching questions about the space-filling of our own local congregation. Why is the church? Where is the church to be? What is its mission? How does it demonstrate the love of God in preparing man to live in the whirling vortex of change?

A town in Appalachia was threatened by the leisure explosion. A large recreational dam promised to bring new tourists and industry into this quiet sylvan community. To protect themselves from the invasion of change the residents simply removed all highway signs that pointed to their town. Thus they pretended that change does not exist. What is the ministry of the Christian congregation which takes up space in that little hamlet? How does it help the people of that community to face up to change?

Change hurts some people, sometimes necessarily, sometimes needlessly. How does a congregation decide whether God's will for them in specific issues of change is to implement, resist, or interpret? It is difficult to establish rules that will fit all occasions and situations, but there are essential assets available within every Christian community. By making use of such resources, the congregation can decide how best to help the larger community within which it ministers, and then can translate its decisions into action.

Christian education, according to a much-quoted statement of objective, is "rooted in the Christian community."[1] This means, among other things, that the congregation educates by its life style. It prepares persons for life amidst change by validating *wholeness.* In so doing it affirms the *whole world,* the *whole life span,* and the *whole person.*

SEEING THE WORLD AS A WHOLE

When the congregation affirms the wholeness of the world, it is recognizing that God is at work in all of life. God calls his people not just to gather in houses of worship, but to live outside the walls looking for the places where he is at work. They are to try to understand his purposes, helping to support these purposes and to oppose those forces which would thwart them.

How many congregations really affirm the wholeness of the world? The very failure of many churches to challenge and hold many segments of the population, whether young or old, blue-collared or white-collared, reflects a loss of wholeness in the church today. Some have lost their appeal to the fringe groups, and others have become fringe groups themselves. To make this question personal, what is your own church fellowship doing to include people of all kinds—the serious-minded, the revolution-oriented, the highly cultured, the uneducated, the wealthy, the poor, the white, the black? To admit the fragmentation of congregational life is not to fail, but rather to accept the challenge to move vigorously in expanding the limits of our concern.

One of the most effective ways in which the congregation may affirm the wholeness of the world is through corporate worship. The worship experience is the response of the creature to the Creator as the congregation acknowledges its dependence upon the resources made available to it by a loving God. The Bible demonstrates that God's community in both the Old Testament and the New recognized its dependence on him. Worship, whether private or corporate, whether unstructured or highly liturgical, always begins with God and points to him. It continually offers the opportunity for crossing points as man, bringing his daily concerns with him, communes with his Creator.

Unfortunately, however, we too seldom avail ourselves of the opportunity for crossing points which worship provides. In fact, we tend instead to lay aside our thoughts of the world as unsuitable for worship. As Richard Jones asks, "How many congregations, when they gather for worship, consider in the heart of the service the voicing of concern for fair housing, or concern for a better hospital in a needy area, or concern for renewal of slum areas, or concern for those living in poverty?"[*] Instead, worship has often been seen as an escape or at least as a retreat from the world, perhaps because we have thought of our Godward relationship as a purely private and essentially ego-centered affair. We have missed the full power which is possible through worship because we have limited the dimensions of its outreach.

The New Testament church shared many tensions and temptations like those of today, but those early Christians, by the very dynamics of their life of faith, were prevented from divorcing their private faith from their private practice. It took many hundred years of history to force a wedge between personal belief and public conduct. The emperor Constantine started the separation by establishing Christianity as the official religion of the Roman Empire, thus pulling the teeth of its prophetic function. This spiritualizing process continued to develop in the intellectual vacuum of the Middle Ages. In modern times the emergence of philosophical movements such as rationalism and personalism have contributed further to the emphases on a religion that deals first and almost exclusively with one's intimate life. Such a religion is wholly inapplicable, almost deliberately so, to the public concerns of life.

Worship ought not to allow for such an escape from this world's pressing needs. Indeed, it cannot! If man is to meet his Creator in the worship experience, then the creation—the material world—must be deeply involved in man's acts of adoration, confession, and thanksgiving. If man is to commune with God, the Father of our Lord Jesus Christ, then man must be in communication with this world for which Christ died (John 3:16; 2 Corinthians 5:19).

Why has so much of our worship been an *escape from* rather than a *preparation for* the strains and pressures of this world? In many business offices and industrial plants there is a cynical movement of a minor order known as the TGIF Club ("Thank God It's Friday"). Christians, in a very different spirit, are called to be members of the TGIS Club ("Thank God It's Sunday"). They welcome the first day of the week as an opportunity to be propelled forward by the experience of worship into the business of the next six days. Rather than a halfhearted expression of thanks that a week has ended with escape into the sanctuary, the Christian gives a rousing cheer that God enables him to enter a new work week with all its possibilities for either good or ill.

If you are tempted to think that for the church to affirm the world as its concern is just so much theological gobbledygook, read these words written to the author in a personal letter by a scientist holding an important administrative post in the graduate school of a leading state university:

> Joe, we have a very interesting and intellectually active Sunday school class here. I often leave the discussions with a basic worry. It is an uneasy feeling that most of this is an intellectual exercise, and that the church in general is not a very effective channel for coping with the real meat-and-bone issues of our society. If this is correct, then I as a church member am partially at fault. It seems to me that, with rare exceptions, the church deals with "safe" issues.
>
> I think that in terms of any particular social issue, we need to ask two

sequential questions: (1) Do we as Christians *have any* responsibility? and (2) If yes, what do we do to implement it?

The second question can involve widely divergent opinions on ways and means. I would not be concerned about that if the answer to (1) were a clear yes. Unfortunately, church groups often seem to limit their "yes" to those points on which (2) is not likely to create any arguments. This can be done by sticking to trivia close at home and by supporting the missionaries who can handle the major issues at a safe distance—all highly impersonal. Or even worse, one frequently encounters a denial that major problems even exist.

I usually feel more cynical about this on Sunday afternoon after the Sunday morning class discussion. I sometimes feel that if a person is serious about making a difference in our society, he can work more effectively through various civic and social welfare groups than through the church.

If this is true, then it means that I, and all other church members, have a serious responsibility to find ways for the church to recognize the demands of our social problems, and to be more effective in its response to them.

Here is a lay person for whom the life of the local congregation in its worship, education, and outreach means a great deal. Reared in a Christian home and educated in church schools, he has heard the commissioning words of Jesus. He is ready to go into the world to tackle the "real meat-and-bone issues." These begin at his very doorstep and extend clear round the globe. Will his fellow members sense his concern and respond to his challenging question? To be Christian, worship and education must share the reality of this secular world, the whole of it.

MINISTERING WITH ALL AGES

A second affirmation of wholeness the local congregation needs to make is its concern for the entire span of human life. Evelyn Underhill has expressed this unity in these words:

> Since everyone, whatever his vocation, is obliged to reproduce the common curve of human life in its passage through time—to be born, to grow, make choices and accept responsibilities, form some human relationships, take some place in the social order, to meet hardship, difficulty and disillusion, to suffer, and at last to die—it follows that all have in this inevitable sequence of experiences something which can be transformed and directed Godwards; or can, in other words, be turned into worship.[4]

Certain issues are basic to any person, whatever his age. God's self-disclosure evokes man's response of faith and love at each stage of man's development. The life span for the individual stretches out:

BIRTH——▶CHILDHOOD——▶ADOLESCENCE——▶ADULTHOOD——▶OLD AGE

Typical of the basic concerns experienced by persons in different ways at various points in the life cycle is sexuality. Although this factor remains a constant part of one's self-identity throughout life, it is constantly undergoing some change. For a preschooler the question may be just one of curiosity as to how and why he is like or different from a person of his own or the other sex. Later childhood raises the concern of what it means to be a son or daughter. Adolescent years bring into sharp focus the question of how to express one's masculinity or femininity. Older youth deals with sexuality from the perspective of selecting a life mate. Marriage calls for further interpretation of male and female roles, and parenthood introduces the problems of men and women in relation to their children. Finally, the later years may call for reconsideration of the meaning of masculinity and femininity as the reproductive powers recede.

New curriculum materials presently being developed by a cooperating group of Protestant communions have Miss Underhill's principle of the "common curve of human life" built right into them. The result of seven years of curriculum design development, the concept of "persistent issues over the life span" has been used in developing resource materials for teaching-learning possibilities.[5]

It may be helpful to see an example of how the congregation's educational ministry specifically applies to the crossing points across the age span. From the large number of illustrations possible, let us select one. We are aware that life at all ages involves experiences of daily routine. For many people routine offers security, but it also may lead to boredom and meaninglessness. The good news for persons all across the life span is that routine takes on worth and meaning in light of God's purposes for man.

The little child early discovers that routines of sleeping, eating, and going to nursery school are necessary parts of life. Through love he may experience the presence of God in these repeated events, and he may be moved to respond by expressing affection toward persons recognized as helpers with his daily routines.

In the elementary years the child's relationships widen, and he looks for more opportunities to sharpen and use his creative skills. But the more involved he is in wider social patterns, from home to school to church to community, the more routines he has to deal with. Don't forget your lunch box! Line up for recess! Take out the trash! Is your homework done? Here comes the bus! Don't forget your Scout dues! He is called on to manage these routines so that they help rather than hinder his activities. With the support of discerning parents and teachers, the child may begin to comprehend that what he does in these and other day-by-day activities is a way of responding to God and serving him. He may even come to see the pattern of his life as related to the larger plan and routines within which God has set life.

Teen-agers are also involved in daily routines. Can they respond with a creative attitude in the rhythm of work, leisure, and rest? Periodic release from classroom schedules, as well as rebellion against routines that seem meaningless, are part of the teen years. Young persons require assurance that what they are doing is useful and meaningful, as well as insight that God is present in every area of life. As they assume responsibility for developing their abilities in stewardship, they may accept responsibilities for the routines involved in maintaining a home. They may learn to distinguish between forms of self-expression which are beneficial and those which injure people and destroy things.

The adult faces much day-after-day routine. How can he deal creatively with monotony and the frustration it breeds? Supported by the gospel and the life of the congregation, he may see the necessity of choosing wisely the routines that make up his life. He will seek constructive means of providing for some freedom from the daily grind. He may cultivate an attitude of curiosity, wonder, and inquisitiveness. He may also compensate for the boredom of routine by finding satisfying experiences in recreation, the service of others, the creative arts, hobbies, and other activities. And, especially important, with the support and guidance of the gospel and its community, he may seek ways of imparting greater meaning and creativity to his daily work, even to the extent of changing jobs or working with his supervisor to remake his present job into a more creative expression for his human capacities.

Throughout these various stages of life, this one common issue which man faces throughout his lifetime, namely that of handling daily routines creatively, is intersected repeatedly by the gospel, each time at a different level and with meaning more appropriate to the increase of experience and maturity. The same principle would apply equally with respect to other persistent life concerns.

AFFIRMING THE WHOLE PERSON

A third point at which the affirmation of wholeness is made by the Christian congregation is the wholeness of the person. Here is a point of particular need in our day of vast social change. The many powerful forces of today such as urbanization, mobility, cybernation, and shifting moral standards are bewildering to many people. As they find themselves living under heavy pressures and among strangers, a quiet terror mounts in them. Alienation becomes total in an individual who, accustomed to living among people who know his name and what he does, moves to a new situation where he finds each day spent amidst a nameless horde. "I am with all these people, and yet *nobody* cares about me or even knows my name."

In this increasing tide of depersonalization the Christian congregation is called upon to affirm a person as one who is known, respected, and needed. The various activities undertaken in the normal life of a parish bring persons into direct communication with each other. When such contacts bear love, respect, appreciation, and understanding, persons feel strengthened. Such qualities are essential if the identity and personhood of the self are to develop fully. A psychiatrist has used Martin Buber's *I and Thou* to illustrate the urgent necessity for a congregation to translate ideals into ways we relate to one another:

> What Buber did in *I and Thou* was to establish the theological validity of a psychological principle. Buber contended that self-concern does not provide self-fulfillment. We become real, full selves only when we relate to others, he declared, for it is only through the reaction of others that our own existence is confirmed. . . . *We* cannot really be unless our being is affirmed by others, and they will not affirm us in a manner that makes us sure of our own existence *unless we affirm them in a manner that totally acknowledges them for themselves.* . . . The terrible discourtesy of thing or token relationships minus the element of this grace is what frightens so many people when they come to large cities or visit towns in which their way of speaking is unfamiliar.[6]

In its own interior life as a church family, the congregation is challenged to draw lines of love that include all. Sometimes congregations fail most miserably within their own immediate relationships. Stop now to ask yourself: How does my congregation think of children? How do adults relate to the youth of our congregation? Do we merely tolerate them? Or just ignore them?

A public school system lost a school principal suddenly in midyear, and the administrators appointed an excellent classroom teacher as his replacement. A few days later, therefore, the children of this teacher's second-grade class came to school one morning only to discover, to their great sorrow, that their beloved teacher had been permanently transferred to a school at the other end of town. The class never recovered from the shock and disappointment. The fact that this event occurred in a public school should not obscure the point. The importance of these children as persons was denied by the crudeness with which the action was taken. When adults are thinking about the education of children, youth, or senior adults, whether in public school or in the church or home, careful consideration must be given to the interests and personhood of those in the group.

How, then, do we affirm the *whole* person? David Evans has answered in terms of the adolescent:

> . . . the church's nurture must be "now" oriented. Youth must be accepted for what they are now, as well as for what they can and will become.
>
> . . . youth must be accepted as full members of the church today, not as members in training. They are entitled to this position by virtue of their baptism. . . . Youth need to be called upon to be themselves, not miniature adults, nor junior deacons, but the younger laity with full rights and privileges. They need to be given every opportunity for service—based upon gifts, not age; on conviction, not personality; on commitment, not experience.[7]

This statement provides an excellent example of the church as a slice of life that includes all ages in a living experience. If the congregation is to be the expression of the gospel to a wider community, each age must contribute of its own wealth of talents to the needs of others. Mr. Evans continues: "Youth are in need of the maturity and experience of the older laity. At the same time, the older laity need the idealism and dreams of youth. Bringing the two groups together for across-the-generations thinking and commitment will enhance the witness of the Christian community."[8]

A personal experience of the author serves to illustrate the rich benefit of such a youth-adult dialogue in the affirmation of personality:

> In our local church school a high school senior and I were teamed as teachers of a dialogue discussion group that included both adults and young people. He and I met each week to prepare the lesson. Using the discussion technique, and an occasional session involving role-playing and other dynamic interpersonal experiences, we soon found that neither the young people nor the adults had any inhibitions about entering into the dialogue.

Life together in a local congregation teaches of God's love as together we say "yes" to the whole of human personality. Love becomes real when the Christian community through its activity and relationships communicates to a person: "Yes, you do matter. We are deeply sensitive to you as a person. We are concerned for who you are and what you desire to be."

EDUCATING FOR MISSION

In light of the responsibility of the local congregation to prepare its members for their mission as Christians living in the world, what are some of the things that we may expect to happen in the educational ministry of the local church?

1. *All members of the congregation, all persons in a family—in short, the total community—will be studying closely related matter at the same time.* New curriculum resources being prepared by several Protestant communions are built on a three-year cycle of theological perspectives, each of which is of central concern to the entire church for that year:

Knowing the Living God
Responding to God's Call to Live in Christ
Being the Community of Christian Love

As persons advance through the various departments of the church school, they encounter the same theological perspective every three years, but on each occasion the perspective will be related to the meanings and experiences of that age level.

Printed curriculum materials will have content suited for the learning abilities of particular age groupings. Thus Mother and Father will be dealing with subject matter in the adult classes related in content to what the senior high daughter and the junior high son will be studying at their levels. The youngest daughter, in the elementary grades, will be studying comparable material at her appropriate learning level. The congregation, as well as the family at home, can share in talking about a common interest in the material studied that day.

2. *The pastor will become a teacher of teachers.* New curriculum resources offer him this definite role, as a yearly perspective book is made available for study under his guidance. Through the training sessions which he shares with the teachers, he helps them to explore both the content of the Christian faith and its relation to the life style of the Christian, with particular reference to the year's theological perspective.

To say that the pastor is the teacher of teachers does not mean that he now assumes new administrative responsibilities. In most churches these are presently assigned to a board of Christian education, director of Christian education, and church school superintendent; and they should remain there. The pastor as teacher of teachers has the responsibility for interpreting the gospel by helping to bring the year's perspective to life as he shares with the teaching staff in a caring, loving, supporting, and redeeming relationship. Crossing points may emerge in a climate of openness as he helps the teachers to discover new meaning and relevance between the gospel and present life situations.

In this special teaching role the pastor avoids the danger of assuming that the truth of the gospel has been "settled once and for all." He is *not* to be the dispenser of revealed truths; if rigid doctrinal answers to "set" questions are what we want, we would do better to get printouts from a computer. Rather, the dialogue promised by the pastor's role as teacher of teachers allows for the creative interaction of pastor and people, and leaves room for the work of the Holy Spirit.

A bonus for pastor and congregation alike is the possibility of his further interpreting the perspective through sermons on its main ideas and crossing points. By so doing he finds subject matter for a series of planned preaching, and the congregation gains additional grist for dinner table and classroom discussions.

3. *Church school classes will develop into dynamic teaching-learning groups.* By exploring the perspective in training sessions with the pastor, the teacher will be helped to think through its focus and content as it applies to his group. Curriculum resources will provide further help with regard to content and will also suggest specific ways in which the teacher can prepare for an educative event that can be translated into real life. The curriculum plan will encourage spontaneity by allowing for the maximum of creative participation by the teaching learner and the learning teacher.

Effective teaching in such a group is somewhat like alternating electrical current. You will recall that alternating current reverses its poles regularly, whereas direct current flows constantly in one direction. Much teaching in the past seems to have been of the D.C. type, but more A.C. is what we need. Even the lecture method can become more A.C. than D.C. in the hands of an unusually skillful teacher.

In the new curriculum planning, the teacher is seen as a person who gives of himself as he seeks to assist learners in their study and investigation of the Christian faith and its applications to life. He helps guide them through the five learning tasks of listening, exploring, discovering, appropriating, and assuming responsibility in light of the gospel. If the group is small (preferably eight to fifteen members, the best size for significant thinking and serious talking), it will encourage involvement, decision making, and responsible response.*

4. *Education will occur in a variety of settings.* Teaching-learning groups may meet at almost any time or place. The church school is a basic element of the congregation's teaching ministry. As such, it provides a balanced and comprehensive program aimed to cover the total spectrum of the church's educational ministry. Its gathering in the church building on Sunday morning is the more familiar setting, but some church schools are now meeting at other hours and on other days of the week. Some of these attempts to move away from the traditional pattern have proven to be of worth.

Other settings with which the church has had successful experience include vacation church schools, day camps, programs of weekday religious education, youth and adult groups of great variety, church-in-home groups, campus student-faculty groups, men's groups, women's groups, and many others.

5. *The value of meditative thinking will be rediscovered.* To understand what meditative thinking is, we need to contrast it with calculative thinking. One writer who has helped to draw this distinction is the existentialist philosopher Martin Heidigger. We can think through needs of consumers and the manufacture of products and we can plan ways to induce the consumption of goods, Heidigger points out, but this is not the most significant kind of thinking. He writes:

> Whenever we plan, research, and organize, we always reckon with conditions that are given. We take them into account with the calculated intention of their serving specific purposes. Thus we can count on definite results. . . . Calculative thinking computes. . . . Calculative thinking is not meditative thinking, not thinking which contemplates the meaning which reigns in everything that is.[19]

This philosopher rightly reminds us that we need both kinds of thinking, calculative and meditative. Meditative thinking, however, is conspicuously absent from the contemporary scene. In these times of change we need it badly, but the very nature of change makes time for reflection exceedingly rare. For this reason the community of faith, which has a rich tradition of meditation and reflection, must provide a context for affirming the whole of the thinking self.

FROM RENDEZVOUS TO RESPONSE

Change demands flexible response. How can we help to bring into being personalities elastic enough to respond to change—and yet not so thoroughly flexible that every new fad, every public whim has them bouncing around like amoral yo-yos?

Dante, in the *Divine Comedy,* describes the vestibule of hell as filled with poor souls running to and fro, ceaselessly rushing around in a never-ending frenzy of purposeless motion. These are the people denied entry both to heaven and to hell. These tortured beings are the people who have always avoided taking sides. Living neither for God nor even for the devil, but only for themselves, their lives have been totally devoid of meaning.

The danger for modern man lies here. If man constantly adjusts and adapts his life course without some North Star by which to guide, he lives in mortal peril of losing his soul in the constant shifting. Yet if man refuses to make the accommodations necessary to meet change, he is likely to break in the process. Flexibility must join with decisiveness. Decision, in turn, must be related to the ultimate. How do we keep flexibility from becoming over-accommodation, and decisiveness from turning into rigidity?

Setting long-range goals helps us to measure our intermediate and short-range objectives. A Christian who asks, "What is God's purpose for creation and for mankind?" is beginning the quest for a lifelong goal. Aided by such ultimate and universal standards, he is better equipped to be both flexible and decisive. As he continues to ask, "Finally, what really matters?" the Christian measures whether his response to change is a wishy-washy going along with the crowd or a deliberate step in the direction he has established for his whole life journey.

9 EDUCATION FOR LIVING IN A TIME OF CHANGE

EFFECTIVE LIVING requires continual learning, and learning demands readiness for change. But how much do we change? And when? As we move into the new, how much of the old do we take with us and how much do we throw away? What kind of Christian education can best help persons to respond adequately to questions never asked before and to situations never faced before? How can a congregation's board of Christian education best provide an educational program that is appropriate for times of great change?

Questions like these are not answered simply. The task is a big one. And yet we know that the church's educational ministry *must* equip persons to live as Christians in this age when new ideas and problems are emerging at an increasing tempo. Curriculum that provides flexibility for today's and tomorrow's changing times is needed; yet it must be rooted in an unchanging foundation and directed toward cosmic goals. Only such a curriculum can deal with the persistent life issues of modern man as he stands at the crossing points.

What is curriculum? When we add up all the planned learning experiences provided by the church to equip its members for relating effectively and redemptively to all of life, the sum total is curriculum. Obviously this definition includes much more than the printed materials used by the teacher and learner, for all the elements of the Christian education process and program are included. *The curriculum is what actually happens in a particular teaching-learning situation.*

The content of curriculum rightly begins where Jesus' commission directs us—in the church as mission. Curriculum has to do with man's relationships in human community, his growth in the Christian faith, his life in obedience or disobedience to his Father-Creator, his living-out his calling on earth, and the promise of the Christian hope in which he may abide now and always.

THE CURRICULUM PLAN

A distinction is thus drawn between the curriculum and *the curriculum plan,* which is carefully prepared by a denomination to help teachers in local educational settings to develop teaching-learning experiences. Such a plan has a common over-all life span design for all settings. The design is adapted for the different age-groups through the various curriculum resources with which the teacher begins his preparation. The curriculum plan offers a carefully thought-out procedure by which the content of Christian faith is related to the interests of the learner at his particular level of development. It does not create crossing points; it only indicates the regions where they are most likely to exist in various life situations. In its total design affecting all age-groups and all settings, the curriculum plan affords opportunity for all sectors of the congregation to support the teaching-learning experiences of the various groups.

To the resources of the curriculum plan the teacher adds all that he knows about the potential learners in his group, as well as all that he can invest of his own personality and his insight into the gospel. This combination of ingredients, under the guidance of the Holy Spirit, allows an effective teaching-learning experience to develop. The more the teacher adapts the available resources to the needs of his particular teaching-learning group, the more the learners gain of personal value, and the more the teaching itself becomes real and effective.

The new curriculum plan, designed to strengthen the complete teaching ministry of the Christian community, draws upon the wisdom of present-day secular studies wherever they are helpful. The insights of psychology, for instance, have provided Christian educators with a growing understanding of persons and their needs. One of these insights is called the *field of relationships,* a concept which recognizes that in life a person finds himself related to God, man, nature, history, and even himself, in certain specific ways which must be recognized and considered. The thrust of the gospel has a special meaning for each individual in terms of his special field of relationships.

Another important insight is that of the significance and processes of small groups. Use of small groups allows increased understanding of the ways in which the principle of "two or three gathered together" makes possible the ministry of reconciliation as well as the increase of knowledge. We are also learning more about one-to-one communication—how each person can better hear the things that the other is really saying.

Social scientists are contributing much to our understanding of Christian education as we minister to and through social structures. They help us to see how people organize their society, including businesses, families, neighborhoods, and countless other formal and informal relationships. All this is relatively new knowledge, and designers of curriculum plans are drawing upon these insights to help communicate the faith to new generations.

In the field of general education new theories as to how people learn are constantly emerging and being tested in actual use. Christian educators are extremely alert to such developments and are usually ready to adopt new methods as they become proven. In fact, in certain fields they have been the pioneers (outdoor education and group work, for instance). The new curriculum reflects these and other current ideas in education.

The idea of learning tasks, as used by Christian educators in present-day curriculum planning, was adapted from the secular educators' concept of developmental tasks. These are the tasks any person must take on at a certain stage of his development in order to move with maturity into the next stage. Although by definition there are no specific Christian developmental tasks as such, there are Christian ways of handling certain of the regular developmental tasks (see p. 70).

THEOLOGY IN THE CURRICULUM

The theology which undergirds new curriculum developments is based squarely on the Bible, reaching deeply into both the Old Testament and the New. The Bible is understood as inspired by the Holy Spirit and as providing a basis for judging nature and history. Biblical interpretation is further enriched by the fertile theological thought that characterizes our own century, which some dare compare to that of the Reformation period. The traditional Christian message is being asserted in terms appropriate for the present revolutionary age, and we need to be aware of what is being said.

To be specific, the new curriculum developments depend heavily on God's self-disclosure, especially as the Scriptures bear witness to it. Though we can trace his revelation both in history and in nature, the supreme expression of his ultimate authority is seen in Jesus Christ, God's only Son and man's only Savior.

The promise and covenant of the Old Testament finds fulfillment in Jesus Christ. Thus an understanding of both Old and New Testaments is essential to the witness of God's unfolding purpose: God's salvation of men. We see that the freedom with which God invested man has been abused. The rebel has marred the image in which he was created, and his misuse of this God-given freedom has brought about the condition of sin. But God has overcome this bondage through the reconciling life, death, and resurrection of Jesus Christ. The work of the Holy Spirit in the witness of the church gives evidence that God continues to confront man and judge his sin. Calling man to repent, God offers in Christ a new life of freedom and wholeness.

The church constitutes the body of Christ, who is its head. What is the church, if not a company of believers who have acknowledged themselves to be sinners, have accepted the forgiveness of God, have entered by baptism into the ministry of reconciliation, and now promise to serve him in obedience and love? The church today is called to a servant ministry in the world. Such servanthood is demonstrated by Jesus Christ, who stooped to perform the menial tasks of a slave. Supported by worship and nurture, the servant people move to serve and witness both within and outside the gathered congregation. Because they have experienced the redemptive and transforming power of God's love, they go into all the world to declare by word and deed the good news of what God has made possible for all mankind in Jesus Christ. The ministry of the church, when dispersed, becomes effective both in its members' personal relationships and in the structures of society. [1]

EDUCATIONAL CONCEPTS IN THE CURRICULUM

The new curriculum resources have not only a theology but also an educational philosophy. One of the most significant parts of this philosophy is the idea of the crossing point, which assumes that God's self-disclosure can be discovered in the life of the learner when that learner has arrived at a level of readiness appropriate for the new learning (see Chapter 5).

The philosophy underlying the concept of the crossing point can be put plainly: Information and experience must be closely linked, for information without experience is soon forgotten, and experience without information is wasted effort. This principle is illustrated in an unfortunate event narrated by a minister of Christian education. He had gathered a group of teen-agers to pack clothing for refugees. After hours of hard work, one of the young persons suddenly asked, "Would you mind telling us what we are doing and where this stuff is going?" The minister had the facts; the young people had the experience. Each needed both—information and experience.

The concept of experience is in itself another key idea. The teaching-learning experience assumes that it is possible to plan and organize a situation in which the learner can discover the content of the Christian faith for himself. Involved in experience are content (the facts to be known) and context (the setting in which the experience can happen). Experience fortifies knowledge.

In the philosophy of this curriculum plan the fundamental learning task for the Christian is clear: to listen with growing alertness to the gospel and to respond in faith and love. How is this task accomplished? Through exploration, through discovery of meaning and value, and through personal appropriation of that meaning and value—all in the light of the gospel. This continual process leads again and again to assuming personal and social responsibility expressly in terms of the light which comes from the gospel.

The concept of the field of relationships puts both teacher and learner into an open-boundary situation, for no person can predict the final outcome of any single particular experience. Man's relation to God, to other men, to mankind's history, and to nature make necessary an open, rather than a closed, system. No Christian teacher can assume that he possesses the final answer. Peter assumed that the Hebrew dietary laws in the Old Testament were final and forever binding (Acts 11:5-18). The pressure of Paul and the vision of divine purposes opened up Peter's system of thought and values. Isn't this openness attested to in Jesus' words: "You shall see greater things than these" (John 1:50)? The possibility of such greater things requires an open system for teaching and learning about God's purposes for human existence.

The educational philosophy of the new curriculum represents a major attempt to link a philosophy of teaching with a dynamic theology. The philosophy describes how the learner makes knowledge a part of his own personal thought and conduct, while the theology provides facts to be learned and an experience to be shared. The two go hand in hand.

BUILDING BLOCKS OF CURRICULUM PLANNING

The six essential building blocks of the curriculum plan are objective, scope, perspectives, context, learning tasks, and organizing principle.

The *objective* provides the orientation and the direction for the whole of the curriculum; in fact it might well describe the purpose of the total mission of the church. It further shows how education contributes to that basic purpose. Though neither teacher nor learner can expect to achieve the objective fully, it draws both of them to deepening understanding and greater commitment throughout the lifetime learning experience. It is valid at every level of maturity as persons, aware of God's self-disclosure, faithfully and lovingly respond to it at any stage of their development. The experience of *becoming* a new person, a refreshingly renewed person, never ends.

Another building block is *scope*. This implies the breadth of everything that the church considers valid in its teaching ministry. The scope includes all that follows from God's redemptive action in human history and the consequences for man of this saving work in his total field of relationships. From this broad scope the church derives the content for its curriculum planning. It includes three elements of Christian experience: man under God, man's relation to man, and man within the world.

From an analysis of the scope in the light of the objective come *perspectives*. These provide a means for centering down upon specific ways in which the scope can be meaningfully expressed. A perspective is a selected part of the full scope of the church's educational ministry, designated as the content for a year's work. It provides an approach which allows for depth of insight. The curriculum plan described in this book includes perspectives for a three-year cycle which can be summarized as knowing, living, and serving. Spelled out they look like this:

1. Knowing the Living God
2. Responding to God's Call to Live in Christ
3. Being the Community of Christian Love

OBJECTIVE OF CHRISTIAN EDUCATION

The objective of the church's educational ministry is

that all persons be aware of God through his self-disclosure,

especially his redeeming love as revealed in Jesus Christ;

and, enabled by the Holy Spirit, respond in faith and love,

that as new persons in Christ they may

know who they are and what their human situation means;

grow as sons of God, rooted in the Christian community;

live in obedience to the will of God in every relationship;

fulfill their common vocation in the world; and

abide in the Christian hope.

These three perspectives incorporate various areas of concern about the significance and purpose of life, such as what it means to be a human being, the significance of human history, and the origin, meaning, and destiny of the natural order. They also focus on the work of God, dealing with the nature and meaning of his self-disclosure and the way he has spoken and still speaks to man's search and man's need. The perspectives provide a vantage point for man's personal response to God's self-revelation (what constitutes the life of faith and what it means *to be* a Christian). Discipleship is also included in these perspectives—how we carry out the ethical, social, and service aspects of the Christian life, *doing* the Christian calling in all our relationships in faithful obedience to Jesus Christ. Lastly, these perspectives afford a place from which to study the nature, history, and mission of the church, both objectively and by involvement in its life and work.

Another building block is *context,* which refers to the learning environment in which education is experienced. The context includes the *climate* for learning, a redeeming relationship which should say that we care, we respect, we support, we value you. It also includes the *setting* in which teaching-learning is carried on in church school classes, whether held on Sunday mornings or at other times of the week; also vacation church school, through-the-week released-time classes, small groups in homes, men's and women's church school groups, official boards and committees of the church, and miscellaneous organizations of persons at any or all ages.

Learning tasks constitute the next building block. Because these have been considered at some length both in Chapter 6 and in the present chapter, there is no need to comment further on them at this point.

The final building block is the *organizing principle,* or rationale for relating the components of the curriculum design to one another. In other words, there must be a unifying idea that allows curriculum planners to assemble the objective, the context, the scope (with its perspectives), and the learning tasks into an integrated whole. In a sense, the organizing principle might be considered not so much a building block itself as the mortar which joins the blocks together.

The organizing principle for the curriculum plan to which we have frequently referred in this book is that "each component in the Design is equally important; each must be woven into the teaching-learning experience; each must be related to the others to establish unity and integrity in a curriculum involving the learner as a whole person."

USING THE CURRICULUM PLAN IN CHANGING TIMES

Throughout this book we have been keenly aware of the uprooting nature of change in our day, as well as the continuing lordship of God in times of change. No curriculum resources, however well planned, can be sufficiently flexible to address themselves explicitly to any individual situation of, say, five years from today. Does this mean that curriculum materials should not be published? Only a few Christian educators would hold this extreme position. They would recognize that while current events change as rapidly as the newspaper headlines, there are vast and important areas in the fields of relationships to men, history, and nature which underlie these changes and which themselves are not subject to rapid change.

Thus, curriculum materials must be prepared, and they should be constructed in such a way that they can always be used with relevance in any particular situation. Four qualities in the new curriculum plan make it particularly helpful for the church's educational ministry in a time of change:

1. The use of a common design for all ages and settings encourages an increased amount of self-direction in the teaching-learning group. The local congregation has the assignment of making the material relevant to a particular situation. To a degree it can do this for the whole congregation, across the age span, as they engage in the study of one perspective, seeking to relate it to the critical issues and events uppermost at the time. This procedure allows for dialogue among persons of various ages as well as within any specific age level. The teachers and learners in your own congregation can translate the curriculum plan into a personal and living curriculum related to their concerns and crossing points. The opportunity of teachers and learners alike to chart the direction of their study is increased. The resources essential for teaching and learning are provided through the curriculum plan, but exactly how these should be used to be effective in a given setting is the responsibility of local leadership. Being able to exercise more self-direction in using the curriculum plan will help generate increased capacities for leadership among those who use it for teaching and learning.

2. The new curriculum plan involves serious and systematic study. It would be foolish to suggest that anything less than this is sufficient to prepare servant-ministers adequate to go into a rapidly changing world. Each year a perspective book will guide the congregation in a

depth study of the curriculum focus. Those who neglect its study will find themselves seriously handicapped in both teaching and learning. Along with the perspective book, all age-groups within the congregation will have at their disposal curriculum materials appropriate to their age and interest.

3. In the new curriculum plan, learning is understood to take place at the crossing points where the gospel meets the concerns that persist through life. The gospel is changeless, but it speaks differently to people in different times, places, and conditions of life. For example, freedom in Christ is a changeless concept, but its meaning to a slave in ancient Rome was vastly different from its significance for a person living in modern North America. Both are free in Christ—this good news is changeless—but each is set free in light of his own situation and time in history. Again, the need for self-affirmation is an unchanging need for all ages. Yet the infant's way of having this need met is quite different from that of the college-age person. Though each needs the love which affirms, the method of expression varies with the age of the person. Thus the changeless intersects the changing, often making for new changes in persons and societies.

4. Another unique feature of the new curriculum plan is its concern for persistent life issues that recur throughout the life span of the learner. These have to do with the person's discovery of self and with his relationship to others, to the natural world, and to history. The more man is aware of change, the more these issues persist and come to his attention.

Learnings come alive when the learner himself makes them a part of his own personal growth. Where the results of the teaching-learning experience catch fire, there the fullness of the curriculum is really taking place. The flow of human life is energized through every particle with the power-giving love which flows from God. Curriculum materials are designed to help these things happen.

10 A STYLE OF LIFE FOR THE CHRISTIAN

How ARE WE TO LIVE AS CHRISTIANS in a secular and changing world? More than a quarter of a century ago, when the process of secularization now sweeping the United States was already becoming quite evident in Europe, Dietrich Bonhoeffer identified this question as the crucial issue of the church.[1] Persons currently involved in the church's teaching ministry are finding more and more that Bonhoeffer's prophetic observation is accurate for our time. If we are to provide for Christian nurture in the church and in the family, the most effective teaching-learning experiences we can offer will be those which demonstrate a style of life that answers the question "What does it mean to be a Christian today?"

Action, not words, is the language through which Christianity makes its message understandable to those outside the community of faith. The world is not tuned in to the verbal messages and pronouncements of the church. Sermons and confessions of faith are so much gobbledygook to those who do not already understand and accept them. The questions Canaan is asking are not necessarily the ones Zion is answering. What Canaan awaits is the demonstration that Zion's professed faith makes it possible for the faithful few to live more fulfilling lives. Christians will be listened to if they clearly show that they dare live according to their faith in the midst of change. Their confidence will show through. Their very style of living will proclaim that God is the ruler in the whirling vortex of change.

DEVOTIONAL RESOURCES FOR CHRISTIAN LIVING

The Christian style of life is interlaced with devotional experiences in which the believer draws upon the great spiritual insights of the ages, and by these he is empowered to go into the secular world and live as his faith commands. The Psalmist said, "Seek the Lord and his strength, seek his presence continually" (Psalm 105:4). How realistic is it for modern man to "seek the Lord"? In a day when he is being told by some that "God is dead" and by others that all morality is variable, can he seriously seek after the Lord of righteousness? Has modern man lost his capacity to know God? Is he playing meaningless games as he tries to come through prayer and thanksgiving into the presence of the Eternal?

Psalm 73 is typical of the devotional resources which can help us to recognize and express some of the problems we face as we live in what often seems an alien world. It has been said that this is the same psalm that was recited before dawn in the catacombs of Rome by slaves who had discovered in Christ a new style of life vastly unlike that of the culture which surrounded them.[2] Harold Bosley comments: "Whenever I read the 73rd Psalm I find myself wanting to make it required reading for at least two kinds of people: those who reject religion as futile; and those whose religion does not mean much to them or to anyone else."[3] Its words "When my soul was embittered, when I was pricked in heart . . ." reflect our own doubts as we find ourselves wondering whether religious living really pays. We identify with the psalmist's despair as he wonders why he should be good when wickedness seems to go unpunished. All around us irreligious (or at best casually religious) people seem to be getting along pretty well— and without the inner torment which Christians experience in tension between high ideals and practical problems.

Such doubt is not a new and radical development in our technological age. What is surprising about modern writers like the "death of God" theologians is that they write as though they are the original discoverers of anxiety! The Bible is full of evidence, of which the 73rd Psalm is only one sample, that man has ever been plagued with severe doubt. But it goes beyond these negative insights. The Bible also bears testimony that man in the past has discovered, or has been discovered by, the God who was presumed absent, missing, or dead. Why should we be any different? Perhaps our modern lostness is due to the fact that we have been expecting to find him, or to be found by him, in the wrong places. Perhaps we expected to meet him in some sentimental setting when he was looking for us in the arenas of the world's action.

The God who makes himself known in the Old Testament is one who takes the secular seriously. We see him dealing with stubborn Pharaohs and faltering Hebrews, with senile kings and rebellious princes, with babies in bulrushes and rams in thickets. We see him meeting men in traveling tents, military feats, and political victories.

The New Testament also bears witness to God's concern with the secular. We are told in the third chapter of John that God loved the *world* so much that he gave his only Son, that everyone who has faith in him might not die but have eternal life—that through the Son the *world* was not to be judged but to be saved. Jesus was probably the most secular man this world has ever known, if secular means to be of one's time, to belong to the age in which one lives. Certainly he was the most secular of the religious leaders of his time. His band of followers included angry rebels (called zealots) with combat knives hidden beneath their cloaks, as well as tax collectors who were nothing more than lackeys of the Roman overlords and were regarded by the Jews as turncoats and traitors. He allowed himself to be seen in the company of women of questionable reputation and even, on occasion, let them anoint his person. No wonder he was forced to acknowledge that his public image was that of a "winebibber and a glutton."

Jesus saw God at work in this world and among these worldly people. He drew his illustrations from this world: the farmer in the field, the housewife at her cleaning chores, the fisherman at his nets. Jesus stood with persons in the midst of all of life, assuring them, as the author of Psalm 73 also gave assurance, that God is always present in spite of his people's doubts. If Jesus was secular, he also knew the need to pray.

Jesus was a man of prayer, and his experiences help us to see the importance of prayer in our own devotional life. Think how many times the Gospel writers tell of his praying: Mark speaks of an early morning withdrawal into the desert (1:35), a late evening retreat (6:46), and the hours of prayer before Jesus' arrest (14:32). Luke writes of Jesus' prayers at the time of baptism (3:21), at the choosing of the twelve (6:12), when conversing with the disciples (9:18 and

11:1), and at the transfiguration (9:28). Many more examples could be listed. The Gospel writers indicate the nature of some of his prayers: thanksgiving (Matthew 11:25), for life's necessities (Luke 11:3), for forgiveness (Luke 17:4), for moral deliverance (Matthew 6:13), for intercession (Luke 22:31f), and for help and guidance in perplexity and despair (Mark 14:36).

In the parables related to prayer, as in his other parables, Jesus calls the listener to respond to the very real stuff of life in this secular existence. His words stop us on the spot, in the place where we actually live. Right here and right now, we are forced to answer Jesus' question: "Who among you?" His abrupt challenge clears away the mist of pious thoughts which so often seems to obscure true prayer. He draws back the veil which would shroud prayer in mysticism. Thus he helps us to understand that prayer is essentially a this-worldly event. We become able to see that the Lord's Prayer has to do with our own world rather than some other; its petitions are for the here and now rather than the by and by. We recognize that in praying with our hearts and lives open to the world we can be receptive to the mighty movements of God's power in the events of this day and this world.

WITNESS THROUGH LIVING

Reinforced by devotional experiences, the Christian implements the convictions of his faith by the way in which he lives in the world. Indeed, his style of life becomes the way the world measures his faith! It is not surprising, therefore, that the world turns a jaundiced eye toward the church much of the time. Christians have often been guilty of proclaiming loudly and acting weakly. But life is more than words, and worldly people expect more from Christians than pretty words. They look for deeds.

A college student attending a religious seminar stated his concern: "I am alienated and I want to get *un*alienated." Do we as Christians really care about this painful concern of his? Certainly not if we are so centered in our own problems that we have no time for those of others. The church that can only say, "Come join us and help us to survive," has little to offer him. Help comes rather from the church which, through the concern expressed for the young person and for others by its very style of living, enables them to feel the strength of its fellowship and of the One who makes life and community possible.

In Jesus we see the cost of the life lived for others. In him we recognize its deep ethical implications. Christ is not just some other-worldly figure, and the Christian faith is not limited to the traditionally "spiritual." The very essence of Christ is to renounce the differentiation between "this world" and "other world." To see God's love as demonstrated in Jesus is to recognize God's power to transform and fulfill our present existence. We are called to life as those who are aware that God, in Christ, has overcome the terrible barriers that threaten all men with alienation. We are to demonstrate that the present-day forces of change need not reduce man to a cipher, for Christ can counteract the dehumanizing tendencies and convert a man into total being and humanness.

By their style of life, therefore, by the way in which they relate to change, Christians are to demonstrate that God's presence enables men to be human as God intended them to be. God does not threaten the humanity of man; this can be threatened only if the final word is that man is alone. If nobody knows him except his fellowman, he is limited by their limitations. If he is responsible to no higher authority than his nation or race or social class, then he is prey to all the tyrannies that infest the modern world. The deepest source of his freedom remains the knowledge that he must "obey God rather than men."

The Christian bases his life style on his understanding of ultimate goals and final purposes. In the last analysis, what does God intend for man? Such ultimates require a vision such as that expressed by the prophet Ezekiel as he proclaimed the word of the Lord (34:25):

> I will make with them a covenant of peace and banish wild beasts from the land, so that they may dwell securely in the wilderness and sleep in the woods. . . . I will send down the showers in their season; they shall be showers of blessing. And the trees . . . shall yield their fruit, and the earth shall yield its increase, and they shall be secure in their land. . . .

Here is a picture of tranquility and security. The sheep graze safely without danger from violent attack; men, women, and children go about their daily routines without the fear of physical violence. All life is without danger. This theme of peace, prosperity, and the common good of all men was the vision not only of Ezekiel but of many of the other Old Testament prophets. The law of the jungle, "kill or be killed," is replaced by a higher and more powerful law. In this prophetic vision the enmity of beast against beast, man against man, is outlawed by God's righteous reign as God's peace *(shalom)* is brought to bear upon the world.

The modern scientist, consciously perhaps, labors with this vision before him of helping to bring into being a better world for all men.

Even the modern corporations that use science and technology to produce salable goods recognize implicitly something of the prophetic vision in slogans such as "Better things for better living through chemistry."

Despite the apparent success of the technical applications of science, this goal of the good of all men appears more remote than ever. Part of Ezekiel's vision is realized. We do live in well-constructed houses and residences. We enjoy well-made, inexpensive clothing. Our worry is weight control, not survival. Science and technology have produced breakthroughs in the medical and educational fields. Nevertheless, the essentials of the prophets' vision remain far short of fulfillment. Indeed, such modern writers as Aldous Huxley, George Orwell, and Erich Fromm describe our age as "anti-utopia," the negation of the vision.

A particularly subtle form of inverted utopia is the LSD cult, a futile attempt to gain the heights of Ezekiel's vision—through chemistry. Its members evince a slavish attitude toward the chemical or drug which promises ecstasy but delivers heartache. The sugar cube is a peculiarly demonic version of anti-utopia because it runs away from the real world instead of trying to make the vision come true.

Despite the pessimism of the anti-utopians, however, old men do still dream dreams and young men continue to see visions of a better world possible in our time! Out of such visions comes commitment to missions or the Peace Corps or Project Hope. People are drawn away from mathematics and into chicken farming; away from Omaha, Eureka, and Manhattan and toward the villages of India, Bolivia, and Nigeria; away from the sophistication and sanitary facilities of the American scene and into the primitive living conditions and resistant-to-change mentalities of alien peoples.

Each one of us, in some moment of sensitivity, has glimpsed this vision of a better world, a world better not just for ourselves but for all—for the alien, the stranger, the one who is different from ourselves. And we know that this vision has been placed before us by God himself, for it represents his will for his world.

CALLED TO BE SERVANTS

As Christians, then, we are called to a servant ministry. We are servants not of a nation, or of a racial group, or of a social class, or of a political party, or of an economic philosophy, or of anything less than the ultimate and supreme value of life. We are servants of almighty God! We are to take seriously the vision of the Old Testament prophets and of the New Testament disciples that man's answers are found in the peace of God, and therefore in whatever can be done in behalf of the disinherited and dispossessed of this earth. Any style of life, to be appropriate to the Christian, must include a keen awareness of this haunting reality.

Prime concerns for all Christians, therefore, would include such matters as the inequity between the affluence of middle-class life in the western world and the austerity of the majority of mankind. A Roman Catholic bishop from Panama said at Vatican Council II: "In Latin America, the church's first task must be to help renovate society, for unless the church is willing to minister to men's bodies, it cannot properly claim to minister to their souls." [4] And another bishop, this one from Germany, told his fellow Catholics they need "to get as worked up about the threat of poverty and hunger as they do about the threat of Communism." [5] Not just Catholics but all Christians need to demonstrate a continuing concern for these conditions, both at home and overseas. They need to stir the consciences of the nations so that national resources will be allocated to meet the problems.

Regrettably, to date the Christian churches have tended to mirror the culture of their environments rather than to stir up conscientious action Here is where they can be agents, rather than captives, of change. Any style of life appropriate to present conditions must evidence an awareness of the great gulf that exists today between the "haves" and the "have nots" of this earth. To do something about man's economic situation will call for true Christian servanthood.

What are some of the qualities that mark the servant style? Here are several to consider: [6]

1. The servant is open toward other persons, accepts them as they are, and is nonjudgmental. He listens sensitively and responds openly to all kinds of persons. He has standards by which he makes his decisions, but he is master of these decisions rather than allowing them to master him. He gives honest and clear feedback to persons in relationships. He holds values but does not load each relationship down with his own value structure. He is not easily threatened by the strange or unknown. He does not withdraw prematurely from even the hostile evidences of life about him.

2. He moves as a free agent, flexible and nonauthoritarian. His absolutes are few but deep and serve him as a rudder serves to keep a ship on an even keel. The servant-minister is able to adapt his mode

of communication to the situation. He is not a "one tune" man. He is open to direction from the Holy Spirit.

3. The servant sees people as persons. He rejects the use of people as tools even for laudable goals, for he is concerned with persons more than tasks. He is alert to feelings and relationships, which hold priority over "jobs to be done." He finds a way to respect personal feelings and still accomplish essential tasks.

4. The servant is patiently at work creating a climate for change. He considers alternatives, tests new ways, endures failures, and is not discouraged by dead ends. Recognizing that change requires experimentation, he is flexible and innovative. He provides help, support, and encouragement for others as they work to accept change. He helps develop trust. He understands his task as enabling others, facilitating their response to change.

5. The servant seeks ways in which to involve persons in the decision-making process as they prepare to meet conditions of change. He encourages the use of personal resources and the self-expression of others. He creatively attempts to find ways to release the full capacities of others and himself.

6. Recognizing that change is to be constituted from within, the servant works to enlist the fullest participation possible from those most affected by the forces of change. He accepts all persons and works for the common good. He recognizes that change is most effective when the decisions are commonly arrived at.

7. Believing that change is educational, he serves as a learner-teacher. Change demands that our skills, understandings, interpersonal relationships undergo constant revision. He is aware that learning occurs more readily when "you act yourself into believing" than when you "believe yourself into acting."

8. He is aware that different people respond in differing ways to the forces of change. He seeks to be sensitive to personal behavior, both his own and that of others, when confronted with change. He tries to recognize and understand the negative responses of dependency, flight, and antagonism as well as the positive responses of consensus and cooperation.

9. He recognizes his interdependence with his fellows and his dependence upon God. Knowing that God's power and love are constantly available, he is willing to venture and risk; knowing of his need for others, he dares to build human fellowship in the face of drastic change.

Such are some of the features of the servant. Obviously not all of them appear consistently in any one person, but the stance as a whole is worthy of cultivation. Many Christians will succeed in attaining it to a very high degree. At any rate their greatest success will come as they strive for more effective ways of ministering to their fellowmen.

THE CHURCH AS A SETTER OF STYLE

The teaching ministry of the church must be such that it visibly illustrates this life style. It allows for experimentation, and it supports and maintains learners as they try, succeed or fail, and try again. The new curriculum plan encourages this climate which nourishes personal development. It does so by taking both life and the gospel seriously. As the learner discovers the intersection in his own experience of the good news and his own needs, he is led to develop a life style that is at once Christian and uniquely his own.

It is natural for individuals and groups to feel threatened in times of rapid change. It is not surprising, then, that today's threats are felt by congregations as well as individual members. How does the congregation face change? Does it throw up its defenses against the nasty questions of college students or the unaccustomed closeness of neighbors regarded as undesirable? How does it come to terms with "black power"? The new curriculum plan encourages the development of personalities able to respond to the challenge of change. More importantly, it seeks to build shapers of change, persons who will see their ministry as creative response to the new conditions which change introduces.

The Christian church in these years of turmoil and change may be compared to a football team. As long as the team stays in the locker room it cannot be what a football team is supposed to be. If it gets up and goes out of the locker room but then only sits on the bench, it still is not fulfilling its purpose. Even if it sends the coach out onto the field, it has not truly faced the opposing team. Not until the players get up off that bench and line up on the field themselves have they become truly a football team.

How does this parable speak to the educational ministry of *your* church in today's changing world? Think carefully before you give your answer. It may cost your life.

NOTES

CHAPTER ONE, LIFE IS CHANGE

[1] Gene Bartlett, address to the American Baptist Convention, Kansas City, Mo., May, 1966.

[2] Eric Hoffer, *The Ordeal of Change* (New York: Harper & Row, 1963), p. 1.

[3] See John W. Gardner, *Self-Renewal: The Individual and the Innovative Society* (New York: Harper & Row, 1964).

[4] Barbara Ward, *The Rich Nations and the Poor Nations* (New York: W. W. Norton & Company, Inc., 1962), pp. 13-16.

[5] Donald N. Michael, *Cybernation: the Silent Conquest* (Santa Barbara: Center for the Study of Democratic Institutions, 1962), p. 14.

[6] "Dilemmas and Opportunities, Christian Action in Rapid Social Change," Report of an International Ecumenical Study Conference, Thessaloniki, Greece, July 25-August 2, 1959, Department of Church and Society, Division of Studies, World Council of Churches.

[7] "Realtor Hits at Socialism," *The Milwaukee Journal,* Friday, October 18, 1963.

[8] For life in modern small towns experiencing the impact of the "urban sprawl" read Arthur J. Vidich and Joseph Bensman, *Small Town in Mass Society* (Garden City: Doubleday & Co., 1960).

[9] For a helpful discussion of the positive possibilities that may result from modern urban life, see Harvey Cox, *The Secular City* (New York: The Macmillan Company, 1965).

[10] For further data see Bernhard W. Anderson, *Understanding the Old Testament* (Englewood Cliffs: Prentice-Hall, 1957), pp. 30, 110, 192; and Norman K. Gottwald, *A Light to the Nations* (New York: Harper & Row, 1959), esp. p. 145f.

[11] See Deuteronomy 8:7-10 for a description of the "good life" of the Hebrew farmer.

CHAPTER TWO, THE LORD OF CHANGE

[1] R. B. Y. Scott, *The Relevance of the Prophets* (New York: The Macmillan Company, 1952), p. 172.

[2] G. Ernest Wright, *The Old Testament Against Its Environment* (Chicago: Henry Regnery Company, and London: SCM Press, 1950), p. 45.

[3] James Muilenburg, "The History of the Religion of Israel" in *The Interpreter's Bible* (Nashville: Abingdon Press, 1952), Vol. I, p. 307.

[4] See Bernhard W. Anderson, *Understanding the Old Testament*, p. 101.

[5] Martin Buber, *The Prophetic Faith* (New York: The Macmillan Company, 1949), p. 135.

[6] Barbara Ward, *The Rich Nations and the Poor Nations*, p. 22.

[7] See Isaiah 42f.; also Norman K. Gottwald, *A Light to the Nations*, pp. 413-426; also Oscar Cullman, *The Christology of the New Testament* (Philadelphia: The Westminster Press, 1959), pp. 51-82.

[8] H. H. Rowley, *The Unity of the Bible* (Philadelphia: The Westminster Press, 1953), p. 66.

[9] *The Church's Educational Ministry: A Curriculum Plan* (St. Louis: The Bethany Press, 1965), p. 40.

CHAPTER THREE, MISSION AMIDST REVOLUTION

[1] Robert Adolfs, O.S.A., *The Church Is Different*, trans. by Hubert Haskins (New York: Harper & Row, 1966), p. 125.

[2] *Ibid.*, p. 130.

[3] T. S. Eliot, *Christianity and Culture* (New York: Harcourt, Brace and Company, 1940, 1949), p. 34.

[4] Denys Munby, *The Idea of a Secular Society* (London: Oxford University Press, 1963), pp. 17, 20.

[5] For another discussion of these issues see Harvey Cox, *The Secular City;* and Daniel Callahan, *The Secular City Debate* (New York: The Macmillan Company, 1966).

[6] See James A. Pike, *A Time for Christian Candor* (New York: Harper & Row, 1964); Joseph F. Fletcher, *Situation Ethics: The New Morality* (Philadelphia: The Westminster Press, 1966); and Howard Moody, *The Fourth Man* (New York: The Macmillan Company, 1964).

[7] In addition to the books cited in notes 4 and 5, see Colin Williams, *Where in the World?* and *What in the World?* (New York: Privately Published, 1964); and Harvey Cox, *God's Revolution and Man's Responsibility* (Valley Forge: The Judson Press, 1965).

[8] John C. Bennett, "The Church and the Secular," *Christianity and Crisis,* December 26, 1966, p. 295. Copyright © 1966 by Christianity and Crisis, Inc.; reprinted by permission.

CHAPTER FOUR, SHAPERS OF CHANGE

[1] Samuel Terrien, *The Psalms and Their Meaning for Today* (Indianapolis: The Bobbs-Merrill Company, 1952), p. 45.

[2] See J. A. Sanders, "God Is God" in *Foundations, The Baptist Journal of History and Theology,* Vol. VI, No. 4 (October 1963), p. 343f.

[3] Alan Richardson, *A Theological Word Book of the Bible* (New York: The Macmillan Company, 1950), p. 14.

[4] J. A. Sanders, *The Old Testament in the Cross* (New York: Harper & Row, 1961), p. 65.

[5] J. S. Whale, *Christian Doctrine* (Cambridge: Cambridge University Press, 1941), p. 40.

[6] William Golding, *Lord of the Flies* (New York: G. P. Putnam's Sons, 1954).

[7] Ernest Gordon, *Through the Valley of the Kwai* (New York: Harper & Row, 1962), pp. 88-89.

[8] Viktor E. Frankl, *Man's Search for Meaning* (New York: Beacon Press, 1963), p. 104. Copyright © 1959, 1962 by Viktor Frankl.

[9] Denis de Rougemont, *Man's Western Quest,* trans. by Montgomery Belgion (New York: Harper & Row, 1957), p. 39.

CHAPTER FIVE, THE CROSSING POINT

[1] Bernhard W. Anderson, *Understanding the Old Testament,* p. 38.

[2] John W. Gardner, *Self-Renewal: The Individual and the Innovative Society,* p. 93.

[3] Viktor E. Frankl, *Man's Search for Meaning,* p. 115.

[4] Gardner, *op. cit.,* pp. 105-106.

[5] John Holt, *How Children Fail* (New York: Dell Publishing Co., 1964), p. 46.

CHAPTER SIX, LOVE IN LEARNING

[1] Martin Heidigger, *Discourse on Thinking,* trans. by John M. Anderson and E. Hans Freund (New York: Harper & Row, 1966), p. 52.

[2] Erich Fromm, *The Art of Loving* (New York: Harper & Row, 1956), p. 26.

[3] John Holt, *How Children Fail,* p. 24.

[4] *Ibid.,* p. 39.

[5] Lois Horton Young, "The Role of Love in Teaching," *Baptist Leader,* August 1963, pp. 15-16.

[6] *Ibid.*

[7] Erich Fromm, *op. cit.,* p. 26.

[8] For some examples see Paul L. Stagg, *The Converted Church* (Valley Forge: The Judson Press, 1967).

CHAPTER SEVEN, CHRISTIAN EDUCATION AS EXPERIENCE

[1] For evangelism and the arts see Richard M. Jones, *Witness Through the Arts* (Valley Forge: Division of Evangelism, American Baptist Home Mission Societies, 1961).

[2] W. A. Visser 't Hooft, *Rembrandt and the Gospel* (Philadelphia: The Westminster Press, 1958, and London: SCM Press, 1957).

[3] Carl F. Burke, *God Is for Real, Man* (New York: Association Press, 1966).

CHAPTER EIGHT, THE CONGREGATION—RENDEZVOUS FOR MISSION

[1] Dietrich Bonhoeffer, *The Cost of Discipleship* (New York: The Macmillan Company, 1959), p. 223.

[2] *The Church's Educational Ministry*, p. 8.

[3] Richard M. Jones, *The Man for All Men* (Valley Forge: The Judson Press, 1965), p. 92.

[4] Evelyn Underhill, *Worship* (New York: Harper & Row, 1957), p. 76.

[5] *The Church's Educational Ministry*, p. 14.

[6] Earl A. Loomis, Jr., *The Self in Pilgrimage* (New York: Harper & Row, 1960), p. 64.

[7] David M. Evans, *Shaping the Church's Ministry with Youth* (Valley Forge: The Judson Press, 1965), p. 41.

[8] *Ibid.*, p. 42.

[9] For further discussion of small groups in a church, see LeRoy Judson Day, *Dynamic Christian Fellowship* (Valley Forge: The Judson Press, 1968).

[10] Martin Heidigger, *Discourse on Thinking*, p. 46.

CHAPTER NINE, EDUCATION FOR LIVING IN A TIME OF CHANGE

[1] This brief description can only sketch the outlines of the theology undergirding new curriculum developments. Official statements of the theological presuppositions can be obtained from denominational boards of education.

CHAPTER TEN, A STYLE OF LIFE FOR THE CHRISTIAN

[1] Conversation between the author and Pastor Eberhard Bethge at The Pennsylvania State University, February 2, 1967. Pastor Bethge was Bonhoeffer's biographer and close friend.

[2] Samuel Terrien, *The Psalms and Their Meaning for Today*, p. viii.

[3] Harold A. Bosley, *Sermons on the Psalms* (New York: Harper & Row, 1956), p. 98.

[4] Robert McAfee Brown, *Observer in Rome* (Garden City: Doubleday & Company, Inc., 1964), p. 93.

[5] *Ibid.*, p. 211.

[6] This list is based, in part, on one developed by Harry L. Moore of the Department of Ministry with Children of the American Baptist Board of Education and Publication, Valley Forge, Pa., January 1967.

5413-4
140